# FROM MURDER TO MESSAGES

## A MOTHER'S JOURNEY THROUGH DARKNESS TO LIGHT AFTER TRAGIC LOSS

### JACKIE SUZANNE RUBIO

DIVINE DESTINY PUBLISHING

# CONTENTS

# INTRODUCTION

This book is a journey through the unthinkable, losing my son, Devyne, and discovering that even death can't silence love.

In the beginning, I'll take you into our world before everything changed. You'll get to know Devyne the way I did, the real him. You'll walk through our imperfect family life, full of love, chaos, mistakes, laughter, and struggle. We weren't polished or spiritual or even particularly healthy back then, we were just human. And that's exactly why this story matters. Because what I've learned is that love doesn't care how broken or messy our lives have been. Our loved ones will find a way to reach us anyway.

Then, we'll move into the darkest part, the shock and pain of Devyne's murder, the grief that nearly swallowed me whole, and the first faint signs that he was still here. You'll see the photos, the synchronicities, and the little *miracles* that I documented along the way.

From there, things start to shift. You'll walk beside me as I find my people, *Helping Parents Heal*, and as I have my first life-changing reading with medium Suzanne Giesemann who gave me undeniable proof that my boy was right beside me. You'll even hear from Suzanne Giesemann, a respected medium who helped me understand what was really happening when Devyne broke through Heaven's door.

Later, the story opens into healing and awakening. I'll share how Reiki, quantum energy, and learning about the chakras helped me understand what was happening not just to me, but through me. I'll talk honestly about the overload of information online, the teachers who helped, and how I began to trust my own direct connection.

You'll also see me stumble. Be real, raw and extremely vulnerable. You'll see the alcoholic, the single mom, the woman who fought through generations of trauma and kept showing up. Because that's the truth, this path isn't about perfection. It's about surrender, about believing that if love is real, it can find us in our messiest moments.

By the end of this book, you'll have walked through hell with me and I hope you'll come out lighter, more open, and more connected to your own loved ones on the other side.

This isn't a story about grief and loss. It's a story about what happens after. About how death isn't the end, and how love keeps showing up, again and again, until we finally believe it.

So if you're standing in your own fire, wondering how to go on, take my hand. We'll walk through it together.

# GETTING TO KNOW DEVYNE MEET MY QUIRKY SON

I really want to share Devyne with you. I hope you'll begin to know him, get a feel for who he was and a glimpse into the kind of kid, and man, he truly was.

Devyne was an interesting kid. He was a really quiet baby. He never fussed or asked for much. When he was a toddler, he loved big trucks, and he loved Bob The builder! He watched adult shows about tractors and construction. He rode his bike so early in age with no training wheels he was such a natural. He was so interested in tires. Like he was truly obsessed with them.

He was eighteen months old, and he crawled underneath my landlord's car, and she backed over him, which was the scariest moment ever. But it left tire marks on his arm that he carried all of his life. And he was okay. He had a broken thumb. That was it. But it's just how curious he was about tires. It's always kind of tripped me out.

Devyne was a good kid, tall, quiet, sensitive, and deeply introverted. In a house full of noise and chaos, he often felt like the odd one out. He connected better with adults than with other kids, and church quickly became the place where he felt most understood. He loved one-on-one time with me, but with four children and a nonstop household, he rarely got the calm connection he craved.

He played football as a kid. When he was in Pop Warner Football, for the little kids, he played so hard that he ended up breaking his ankle toward the end of the season. Even then, his determination and quiet courage were clear, he approached everything with intensity and a deep sense of commitment, even when it hurt.

He loved me deeply and was always softer with me when it was just the two of us. But he struggled with the chaos around him and never quite fit in with his siblings when they were young. Still, as adults, they were slowly finding their way back to each other, reconnecting, talking more, and mending old wounds. They were finally building the relationships they never had growing up.

Let me tell you one funny memory, this one still cracks me up. I realize as the reader this may be a bit shocking, but I want to reveal us, our real story, Devyne's truest nature.

There was a party. An adult party. The kind that Devyne normally would not attend but this time he was there, he was of age, and a handsome boy. One of the women at the party got a little too flirtatious with him, and he was not appreciating it.

At one point, she took a picture of her boobs, pierced and all, and set it as his phone's screensaver.

Well… Devyne didn't say a word about it. But in the morning, when she went out to her car, she found that he'd gone in during the night and changed her radio to the Christian station. And not just that, he'd turned the volume all the way up.

So, when she got in hungover, all she heard was Jesus' music blaring at full blast.

That was how he reacted to seeing her boobs.

Quiet revenge. Full of values. Totally Devyne.

Devyne rarely got in trouble as a kid, except for one time, in middle school.

There was this small, younger boy who was the kicker on his football team. One day, during recess, Devyne saw a group of bigger, older kids picking on him. They had taken the boy's shoe and were throwing it around, taunting him.

Devyne didn't just stand there and watch. That day, and only that day, he came in swinging. He jumped in to protect that boy, fists and all. And yeah, he got into a little bit of trouble for it. But it was the first and only time.

That was Devyne. While a lot of kids his age were sneaking beers, smoking weed behind the school, or chasing trouble just to see how far they could push the line, he wasn't interested. He never got tangled up in any of that. He kept his distance, not in a judgmental way (okay maybe a bit in a judgmental way), but almost like he just knew it wasn't for him. He was steady, grounded.

I think part of that was because of me, because of the home he grew up in. Our world was loud, chaotic, unpredictable. I was drinking, there were always people around, and life often felt risky. Where I leaned into the noise, he leaned into safety. Where I lived messy, he tried to live clean. It was like he carved out his own island of calm inside all that storm.

If he ever did break the rules, it wasn't for himself. It was for someone smaller, someone more vulnerable. He had this way of stepping in when things didn't feel fair, even if it meant taking the heat for it. That was his version of rebellion, defending the kid who didn't have a voice.

He got his first job as a school janitor. He had gone to what they call Youth Corps, where he got his GED, some certificates, and took part in trade school activities. After that, he got hired straight into the Redmond School District as a janitor. We lived about five miles from the school and his first day his bike tire went flat, and he walked the entire five miles to get to work.

He was really, really loved there.

The little kids adored him. He would even participate in reading time with them. There is actually an article written about him. Check it out here: https://bendbulletin.com/2014/06/18/former-redmond-student-comes-full-circle/

The school district loved him so much, after he had been there for a while, they did something really special, they held a celebration just for him. They let him walk down the aisle in a cap and gown. With all the children assembled to clap and to witness his ceremony.

At the time, he was driving a truck that he'd had a little accident in. It didn't have any doors on it. So, the school district went out and bought him new doors for his truck. I mean in a world of school district politics this just doesn't happen.

He was just so loved and so celebrated. People really adored and supported him.

Dev was extremely polite. That's something that struck people about him right away. He carried this quiet kindness that made people notice. That made people care.

It was during this time of his life that Devyne loved Taylor Swift.

He was so funny about it. He cut out a picture of Taylor Swift, taped it to the passenger seat in his pickup, and drove around town like that, with his arm around it, saying he was married to her.

That was Devyne. Serious and religious on the outside… but full of quiet, quirky humor if you knew where to look.

## Meeting Paige

Devyne and Paige weren't strangers when they married. They had known each other since childhood, sitting side by side at youth group. Life carried them in different directions for a while, but when they crossed paths again as young adults, he was twenty, she only eighteen, something clicked.

Devyne had such a strong moral compass, seeing the world in black and white, right and wrong. He was also painfully shy. For all his good looks and charm, he never played the role of a ladies' man. His awkwardness and gentleness made him stand out in a different way, he was someone who waited. He saved himself for marriage, which meant Paige was not only his wife but also his very first partner.

Even as an adult he didn't drink or use drugs. In fact, my own drinking was one of the hardest parts of our relationship. He wasn't comfortable in crowds, while I was the kind of person who always had a house full of people. He would shake his head and say, "Mom, you can't even go to the grocery store without bringing fifty of your friends." We were opposites in that way, and sometimes that was hard for him. But his quietness, his conviction, and his sincerity were at the heart of who he was.

The day his son was born, Devyne did absolutely amazing. I was so proud of him.

I got to be there when my grandson was born. It was a complicated day, he had a medical issue, a pretty urgent one, and had to be airlifted to a bigger hospital in Portland, Oregon. But Devyne handled it all so well.

And the most beautiful memory I have of him, the one that will always stay with me, was seeing him do skin-to-skin with his newborn son.

There was just something so precious about that moment. Devyne was such a big guy, and he had a hard time showing emotion. He wasn't the super emotional type, he was more logical, well put together. But in that moment, with his shirt off and this tiny baby resting on his chest, everything softened.

It filled my heart in a way I can't really describe. It made me so full, so proud, and so completely overwhelmed with love for him.

Meanwhile, his marriage to Paige began unraveling almost as soon as it began. She was controlling, and little by little, she isolated him from his son. The separation happened abruptly, leaving him devastated. For someone who lived by such a strong sense of right and wrong, divorce felt like failure. To make matters worse, Paige quickly moved on to a same-sex relationship, and from that point forward, she often cut Devyne out of parenting decisions.

He carried that heartbreak heavily. He had been through so much already, the divorce, the custody battles, the endless fight just to be a father in a system that always seemed tilted against him. And yet, even in that pain, something in him began to shift.

For the first time, Devyne started to see the world in shades of gray instead of rigid black and white. He began to realize that strength didn't mean carrying everything alone. He was learning that empathy was as important as boundaries, and that sometimes, love required letting go of the hard lines he once lived by.

And in that space of struggle, he started to reach back toward his family. He started to accept us for who we were. When he needed help with his legal battles, I didn't hesitate. I sold my property in Texas, packed up my life and moved to Oregon to stand by his side, physically, emotionally, financially.

I wanted him to know he didn't have to do it alone anymore. That I was there. That he mattered. That I was sober, and real, and present.

We were doing the work and just when he was coming back to life, she took him from me.

He had finally found love. The real kind. The kind that made his shoulders soften. That gave him a reason to come home smiling.

He was engaged to a woman who lit him up from the inside.

She came with a big, loud, loving family, the kind he never wanted to feel part of. I enjoyed this twist of fate and through his relationship with them I saw him changing and being more tolerant of me. They carved out a life together. They were building something, brick by brick, dream by dream.

It wasn't perfect, but it was theirs.

Life was hard, and custody fights weren't cheap. He took a second job to pay the legal bills and drained their wedding savings to cover the fees. He made sacrifices that no father should have to make just to be a father. But he did it so methodically. One step at a time. Because he believed there was a future ahead worth fighting for.

A marriage. A family. A clean slate.

And then, before the vows, before the dress, before the joy, she took it all from him.

He never got to marry the woman he loved. He never got to walk down that aisle or hold his son in peace.

All that beauty, all that rebuilding, all that hope, cut short by fear, by violence, by someone who couldn't see who he really was.

Here is a memory his older sister Dakota wrote.

**Weirdy Beardy**

Growing up, my relationship with my brother was complicated, but as we got older, we built a better friendship. The thing I want everyone to know about Devyne is that he was a huge dork. He made terrible jokes and smiled like a loon when he did. He used silly words and pronounced things in the funniest ways. I even have a tattoo from one of our inside jokes, when people were acting strange, we called them "weirdy beardy."

We used to exchange memes on Facebook or make endless SpongeBob references.

When we lived close by, he'd pick me up to get coffee and we'd sit together, talking about our problems.

Devyne absolutely loved sweets. He would drink syrup straight from the bottle—I caught him doing it more than once. One time, at a diner, he ordered extra whipped cream for his pancakes, and the waitress brought out the whole can. He was so excited, and believe me, he used the entire thing.

My favorite memory of him is from his bachelor party. Instead of a wild night out, he wanted an ice cream bar. We got the works: cones, syrups, toppings, whipped cream. He was so happy, grinning with that same dorky smile, just because he was eating ice cream with the people he loved.

*Devyne at his bachelor party ice cream bar, grinning, of course.*

At his funeral, when it was time for everyone to speak about Devyne, I was worried people would treat it too seriously— that I'd be the only one talking about what a total dork he was. But that wasn't the case. We all shared our own stories about his quirky tendencies and the funny little things he did. The centerpieces were Dr Pepper and candy.

Devyne was a good man who loved life's simple pleasures. He wasn't afraid to be himself or to be silly.

When I think of him, I think of SpongeBob blankets, trampolines, and sugar.

The world is a much darker place without him. I miss him dearly.

As his mother, I am glad that I can still access and share these memories with you, the way he laughed, the ways he moved through the world, the moments that made him Devyne. In sharing them, I honor his life and reclaim a piece of myself that tragic loss tried to steal.

## 2

## THE CALL

Disbelief. Anger. Confusion. Twisted words that brought whole worlds crashing in on themselves. And yet, somehow, a layer of denial so thick it could have made the Nile look like a backyard creek.

They were lying. All of them. Everyone on that call, everyone delivering the news. Liars of the cruelest kind.

Stirring up drama and distress just nine days before Christmas.

There was no way my son, my kind, 6' 4" tall, strong, gentle 28-year-old baby, was shot to death on the porch of his ex-wife's house while trying to pick up his son. That couldn't be real. That couldn't happen to my child. Not to my son, who avoided conflict at all costs. Who walked gently in the world, who always followed the rules.

Unlike me. I've been courting conflict my entire life. If controversy doesn't knock on my door, I go out and hunt it down. But he was different. He stayed in the lines. He played by society's rulebook. He believed in fairness and kept the peace, even when it cost him.

I hung up the phone with my whole-body ringing, an overload of information, emotion, and noise. Every cell in me vibrating with contradicting truths and lies, rage and denial. No officer or hospital had confirmed anything at that moment. No facts. Just this wild, violent, unbelievable news.

Yes, there had been a bitter custody battle.

Yes, I had felt a knot deep in my gut for months.

Yes, her behavior had become increasingly unstable.

But still, he was a good man. A good father. A safe man. He lived in a quiet town. He did everything right.

Rage began to boil under my skin. A darkness I didn't know I was capable of carrying rose and exploded inside of me, spitting fire into every fiber of my being. But then, just as quickly, it dropped out from under me, and I was left with nothing but numbness. This wasn't real. It couldn't be. Someone had made up some dramatic lie. Happy freaking holidays.

Oh God. My Kids

How can I tell them?

Will they be okay?

Will I be okay? How will I ever stay sober now?

Does anyone believe this?

The human brain should not be capable of processing this many scenarios at once. It felt like it defied physics itself. And then, silence.

Mind blank.

Body numb.

I had no answers from police nothing confirmed, and I had a 3 ½ hour drive to make alone. I searched for my keys through the blur. My hand reached down to pick them up, my lucky rabbit's foot dangling from the keychain. A gift from my son and it didn't feel so lucky now.

**The Moment**

Forty-Five minutes into the icy drive, the phone rang again. Quietly My Nephew whispered, "It's true, He's gone."

After the call, my legs barely worked. My body sagged beneath the weight of the truth as it finally settled into my marrow.

Yes.

He was dead.

Yes.

She shot him.

Yes.

He was gone.

Pain shot through my limbs. My head pounded. My heart tore itself apart with such force I could feel my ribs tighten around it like a prison. I rubbed my arms. Hard. Rubbing, rubbing, rubbing, trying to stay here. Trying not to fall into that black abyss that wanted to swallow me whole. Keep your hands on the wheel do not lose control I repeated over and over.

I couldn't let go.

I had to get to my other kids.

They needed me.

And I knew.

Somehow, I knew, my life would never be the same.

Not after that moment.

Not after that call.

**No Open Caskets**

I stood at the front of the funeral home. Holding my Children tight. Trying to square my shoulders like armor. Laying my head on them weeping in a grief no mother should ever know.

"There will be no viewing," the funeral director said, gently but firmly.

Too many wounds.

Too much damage.

Too many bullets in too many places.

All that remained of my son for us to touch and hold was one large hand. They left it out from beneath the quilt that covered the rest of his broken, mutilated body.

That hand had been twice the size of mine—strong, warm, and soft. It had worked long days to provide for his son. It had played piano and tossed footballs. It waved to strangers and served food at the local shelter. It was the hand of a giver, a caretaker, a man filled with quiet goodness.

How could that be the only part left to touch?

How could that lifeless hand be all I had left of my living, breathing, laughing, joking, hilarious, helpful, kind, humble boy?

The weeks that followed blurred into a haze of autopsy reports, meetings with the DA, conversations with law enforcement. I couldn't tell if it was 2 a.m. or 2 p.m. most days.

The fact that my beautiful seven-year-old grandson was in the home during the shooting haunted me every moment of every day.

People often ask me what my grandson saw that night, what he heard, and what he remembers. It's one of the hardest questions, because the truth is tangled in both what we were told and what he later revealed.

He was only seven years old when his daddy was murdered. He was in the house, present, while his father was shot nine times. The story that circulated at first, from police, from his mom, from his other grandma, was that he didn't know. That he was in the bathtub. That he never saw or heard. That the paramedics and police shielded him from everything, even covering his little eyes with a jacket as they carried him outside.

But later, he himself would tell us differently. He said he did see. He said he did know. That night, in his little seven-year-old way, he had witnessed what no child should ever have to witness.

And that's the truth that cut me to the bone.

Because my grandson is no ordinary boy. He is so sharp, so perceptive, wise far beyond his years. He is an exceptional student, the kind of child who notices everything. And he loves me, oh my God, how he loves me, and I love him with every fiber of my being. He never once saw me as the alcoholic I used to be. To him, I am just his grandma, and he adores me.

I often say that being his grandma is the one thing I got right. We have the most beautiful bond. He is my heart. My safe place. My proof that love can be pure.

So, to imagine him sitting in that house, hearing those shots, feeling the chaos, seeing the blood, knowing on some level what had happened, it broke me in a different way than even losing my son did. The thought of his little mind trying to piece together what no child should ever be asked to understand, it haunts me still.

The police tried to shield him, yes. But you can't shield a boy like that. He is too smart, too awake, too attuned. He knew. And that knowledge, that awareness, is another layer of grief we all hold.

In the middle of shock and sorrow, the world kept moving, paperwork piled up, rumors started swirling, and truth got tangled in speculation.

For the rest of the world, the sun still rose, and life moved on, but not for me. I stood trapped in court drama, fully realizing my son was gone. Every thought was jagged, every breath a struggle. The grief was a living thing, clawing through me, leaving me raw and unmoored. And yet, even in that unbearable darkness, what came next would test every fiber of my being, challenge every belief I held.

That's when I first heard about the tape.

**The Tape**

The rumors started almost right away.

That Devyne had kicked in her door. That he was raging, threatening her. That she was scared, and it was self-defense.

But anyone who really knew my son knew that wasn't him. That wasn't Devyne. The Devyne I knew was trying to hold his life together the best he could, even while she was pulling every string to tear it apart.

She kept his son from him. She filed false police reports and obtained rulings that carried real consequences. She distorted the facts until a convincing story existed and, tragically, many accepted it as truth.

I'll be honest, at first, I didn't know what to believe. I was barely breathing. My ears were ringing. My hands were shaking, and when I heard those stories, some sick part of me thought… maybe he did snap. Maybe he just finally couldn't take it anymore.

But he didn't.

He was scared of her. Scared enough to install a dash cam. And that dash cam, that little black box, told the truth no one wanted to say out loud.

He knocked. Calm. No yelling. No threats. No banging on the door.

She opened it.

And she opened fire.

No warning. No hesitation. No words.

Just bullets.

I couldn't watch the tape.

They asked me to. Told me I had a right to. But I couldn't. I still can't.

That video became more than evidence, it became a wound I couldn't look at. A moment frozen in time that I knew would break me in a way nothing else could. Just the thought of it felt like another nail in Dev's coffin, another dagger pressed into my already broken heart. It wasn't only about what the video showed, it was about what it represented. Finality. Proof. A reminder that my son was gone and there was nothing I could do to change it. I carried enough images in my own mind; I didn't need another one forced upon me.

Turning away wasn't denial. It was survival.

But others watched it. Attorneys. Officers. Investigators. People in suits who drank their coffee and nodded like it was just another case. I remember looking at them and thinking, You saw him die. You witnessed my son's last breath. And somehow you still went home, ate dinner, laughed with your kids and slept through the night.

I envied that kind of numbness. And I hated it, too.

People expected rage from me. They expected me to storm the courthouse, flip tables, curse her name. And I wanted to. God, I wanted to. But my body would just sag under the weight of it all. I did not have the energy to feel hate or the space in my heart.

What I felt was something else. I felt sick. Hollow. Emptiness filled my body, and I felt nothing.

I would try to reason with myself to tell myself no one would do this if they didn't THINK they had a reason. But then I would feel so guilty trying to give this woman the benefit of the doubt. I felt like if I did that then I would be betraying my son. MY INNOCENT SON!

But that wasn't the only guilt.

It opened a door. One I couldn't close.

All the memories. All the ways I failed him. All the times I wasn't there. The drinking. The chaos. The messes I made in his childhood that I always thought I'd eventually get the chance to make right. I thought I'd have time. I thought I'd get to show him who I really was, sober, steady, awake.

And the hardest part is I had just begun showing him. By the time Devyne was murdered, I had been sober for two and a half years. I had devoted myself to rebuilding our relationship, and slowly, he was starting to believe in it. He was opening up again, letting me back in, allowing me to be part of his world. I could feel his heart softening, his trust growing. For the first time in a long time, he wanted me to be part of his family.

Before my sobriety, visiting him had always been a delicate dance. If I came to town, he would take his time to come see me. He'd feel me out first, almost like a careful observer, testing whether I was truly sober, whether he could trust me in this space. There was always a pause, a subtle distance, a standoffishness that kept me on edge.

This time was different. The moment I arrived, he met me. No hesitation. He helped me unload my horses, even backed up my trailer without a word of complaint. It was completely out of character for him. Devyne had always measured me, gauged my strength, my independence, my ability to stand on my own. And that day, as the beautiful Oregon sunshine spilled across the fields and the crisp air filled my lungs, I felt a deep relief. Relief that I had made the decision to come, to be with Devyne during this pivotal time in his life. I could see the reassurance in his eyes, he trusted that I was sober, that I was strong, that I could hold my own. It felt like a quiet victory between us, a moment of connection that made me feel seen, capable, and loved.

That's why I sold my house in Texas and moved back to Oregon. I wanted to be close to him, to make sure he had what he needed, attorney money, support in court, a steady reminder that he didn't have to walk this world alone anymore. I wanted him to know, without question, that I was there.

Sometimes quietly, sometimes not so quietly, I stood beside him as he found his strength. I encouraged him to fight for his rights to be in his son's life. To finally stand up to her, the woman who had controlled so much of his world. She dictated every part of their marriage and, even after, every aspect of his relationship with his son. And I wanted him to see that he could rise above it. That he was worthy of being both a father and a free man.

So final. No more time to fix it. No more time to continue what we had just begun. That truth nearly broke me. I would never get to say what still needed to be said. Never show him who I was still becoming. Never continue to see his eyes soften and trust me again.

That's what grief does. It takes away every future version of yourself, every version you had worked so hard to become, every change you had fought for, every promise you made to yourself. All the "not yet" moments, the ones you swore you'd reach someday, are ripped away. And then, in an instant, it's too late. But even in that bottomless pit of regret, something else started to burn in me. A fire. Not the kind that destroys although I had experienced that as well, the kind that refines. It told me, "If you can't show Devyne in the physical, then show the world. Show his son. Show your other children. Become what you weren't. Be the mother now that you weren't then."

Even in the wake of all the chaos, lies, and cruelty, one truth remained unshakable: Devyne was my son. I couldn't change the past, couldn't undo the hurt, and couldn't protect him from everything. But I could honor him. I could honor his life, his spirit, and his son.

I was filled with determination and spiritual desperation, the kind that grabs hold of you and won't let go, to redeem what I still could. To never drink again. To fight for my grandson. To make sure he knew his father's true self, his personality, his gifts, the man he truly was, not the twisted version he was being fed. To be there, really be there, for my three surviving children. It didn't erase the guilt; it just gave it somewhere to go.

Early on, during the custody trial with Devyne's ex-wife and her mother over my darling grandson, I would file into the courtroom, looking at the face of the woman who murdered my son. I listened to her attorney say horrible things about me as a mother, some true, and some completely fabricated. They disregarded the hard work of my sobriety, my women's empowerment nonprofit, and my service in the community. It was, to say the least, a hard pill to swallow.

No matter what I did or how much money I spent, I could not change Oregon law: the killer, the woman who murdered my son still maintained custody and the right to choose where my grandson lived. Even though the murder was caught on video, she was "innocent until proven guilty."

The loneliness, the guilt, the torture of knowing I had not only lost my son to this family, but I was also losing my grandson. He was continually being pulled out of my reach. No matter how much love, devotion, and pure intention I had, he was being taken. His father, and our entire family, was being erased from his life and his memory.

I'm writing this more than two and a half years later, and I have still not seen or spoken to my grandson. The heartbreak is unbearable at times.

But now, when the feelings get so intense, when my very breath feels frozen with grief, I hear the beautiful words of Bob Marley being sung over and over in my mind, in Devyne's voice:

> "Don't worry about a thing, Cause every little thing is gonna be all right."

I remember during the custody case, and in the early proceedings of the murder trial, this lyric would play on a continuous loop. At the time, I didn't even dream that it was Devyne doing it because, honestly, besides the denial that a loved one remains after death, I didn't even know if he had ever listened to Bob Marley in his lifetime on Earth.

But this has become a very important lesson I've learned about souls on the other side, they use what's already in your consciousness, your memories, your energy, to get through to you.

And now, when those lyrics play over and over again, I embrace them. I know it is my beautiful son comforting me, loving me, helping me get through the unbearable pain. Giving me peace and respite from the harshness of my reality and heartbreak.

**Thank you so much Devyne for being so clever.**

I have included the link to the unedited live stream of Devyne's funeral, and it was a hard decision to make. I still haven't been able to watch it myself, but I wanted you, the reader to feel who he was through the voices of the men who stood for him that day. Their words brought pieces of him to life in a way only they could.

*Scan the QR code to watch the unedited service.*

*Devyne's Funeral Service*

3

# THE SHATTERING
# AND THE SIGNS

I need you to know something before we go any further.

The signs came early.

Devyne was trying to reach me almost right away with feathers, dreams, flickering lights, dead car batteries, electronics that didn't make sense. Songs on the radio. Things that seemed like coincidence… but weren't.

But I couldn't see them clearly.

Or maybe I did… but I couldn't let myself believe.

I was twisted.

Twisted in grief.

Twisted in old religious beliefs that told me this kind of thing wasn't real, or worse, that it was wrong.

Twisted in fear.

Twisted in the trauma of losing my son in a way no mother should ever have to endure.

Twisted in disbelief that he, my Devyne, could still be reaching out after death.

The confusion of it all, the pain, the spiritual war inside me, it nearly broke me.

And that inner war didn't just make me suffer… it made me miss the love he was still trying to give. That was the most torturous part.

Not just that he died… but that I couldn't receive the very signs he was sending to show me he never really left.

If you're reading this and you're grieving, doubting, questioning, or awakening, I want to tell you something right now, you don't have to suffer the way I did. You don't have to reject the signs. You don't have to let the world, the church, or your own fear rob you of connection. You don't have to be perfect to receive love from the other side. You just have to be open enough to wonder. That's where it begins.

At the time, I had temporary custody of Devyne's son. It was a complicated, heavy, heartbreaking situation, one I never imagined I'd be in. One that would soon take another turn.

The court case was devastating. I had temporary custody of Devyne's son at first, but then we had to change judges. The new judge upheld Oregon law, which meant his mother kept custody. I cannot even begin to describe what it felt like to walk into that courtroom, grieving the murder of my son while trying to protect my grandson, and hear a decision that left me feeling powerless.

The courtroom smelled like fear. It smelled like betrayal. It felt cold, icy, and utterly unmoved by compassion. Every word, every glance, every decision seemed to echo against the walls like a reminder of what we had lost and what we could not change.

I was asked to leave my home in Eastern Oregon, a five-bedroom house on twenty acres and move to the town where my son had been killed, where my grandson went to school, just so I could try to provide some stability. I had to arrange visits with his mother, the woman who had taken everything from my son. I did it all with as much grace as I could muster, never saying a word in front of my grandson about her, or anyone else, trying desperately to shield his heart from more pain.

The mornings getting him ready for school became small, sacred moments of connection. Each day, he would go through his father's wallet. He'd hold up the driver's license and grin, saying he looked like his dad and therefore should be allowed to drive to school. He would get out his dad's credit cards and proudly tell me what he was going to buy with them. I kept cash in his dad's wallet so that when we went to pizza, bowling, or the arcade, he could pretend his dad was still there, paying for the fun, sharing the experience. Those moments were full of grief, yes, but also joy, glimpses of normalcy, laughter, and the living memory of a father he loved and missed deeply.

But inside, I was gutted. Every part of me ached. Meanwhile, on the other side, recordings and jail tapes showed them encouraging my grandson to call me a lair, to speak against us, to alienate him from his father, from his family, from the love he deserved. Parental alienation isn't just a legal term; it's a daily, living cruelty. And our family was caught in it, left to navigate the sharp edges of loss, betrayal, and grief.

I don't want to hate. I don't want bitterness to rule me. But in that moment, I was raw, broken, and furious at the unfairness of it all.

**The Signs**

For a moment, in the middle of all that chaos and grief and confusion, there was a simple evening.

We were outside playing Frisbee. Just me and his boy. Trying to be normal. Trying to hold on.

We were staying in this older mobile home, and the roof had tires on top, to help prevent lightning strikes. The Frisbee got tossed too high and disappeared up onto the roof. I got a ladder, climbed up, looked around, but it was nowhere in sight. Must've gotten wedged under one of those tires. I wasn't about to go crawling around on that roof.

So, we let it go.

But something in me stirred. As I climbed back down the ladder, I looked up and said, without really thinking, "Hey Dev… if you're out there, can you get that Frisbee down for us?"

I didn't even know if I believed he could hear me. But I said it anyway. A little part of me was just hoping. The next morning, I was getting my grandson ready for school. I opened the door and there it was.

The Frisbee.

Right in front of the car, placed exactly where I'd have to step over it to get in. My heart stopped and I caught my breath. I began to buzz and tingle all over. My brain tried to reason it out, maybe wind, maybe animals, maybe… something.

And then I began to criticize and chastise myself. How absurd I was being. How ridiculous.

But deep down, I knew.

That was him.

That was Devyne.

That Frisbee felt like his way of saying:

**"Mom, I'm right here. I hear you. I see you. I'm still with you."**

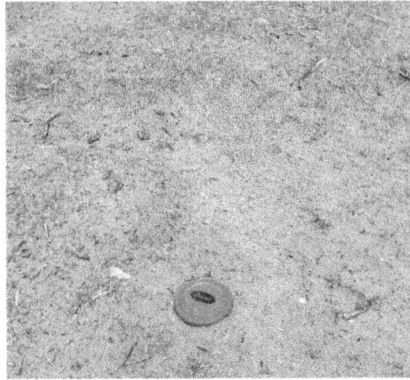

But I need to be honest with you, that moment didn't flip a magical switch.

It didn't pull me out of grief or instantly make me believe in signs or suddenly restore my trust in love after death.

I saw the Frisbee.

I felt something.

And then I spent the next year tearing myself apart, wondering if I had imagined it and the many other signs Devyne sent.

Because here's the truth, I believed other people got signs. I believed other people could talk to their dead loved ones. I even believed that Devyne was trying to communicate with someone. I just couldn't believe it would be me.

Not because I thought the signs weren't real, because deep down, I didn't think I was worthy of them.

I was tortured by guilt. By all the ways I had failed Devyne in life. By the kind of mother I wished I had been but wasn't. By choices I made. By things I didn't do. By the heavy, impossible burden of regret that no one can prepare you for.

How could he possibly still love me?

How could he possibly be sending me gifts, when all I felt I had given him was pain?

That belief, that I didn't deserve to be loved by my own child in spirit kept me in hell for a long time. Even as the signs kept coming. Even as the synchronicities got louder. Even as the undeniable moments of connection kept landing in front of me, just like that Frisbee.

It would take time.

It would take unlearning.

It would take healing I didn't even know I needed.

But that morning with the Frisbee, that was the crack in the wall and Devyne never stopped trying to widen it.

---

Once the courts dismissed the custody case of my grandson, he was taken from my life.

No visitations.

No goodbye.

Just… gone.

My grief got darker.

My hopelessness got deeper.

My guilt and shame, over not even being able to help Devyne's son stay connected to his father or preserve his memories, drowned me in every part of my life.

But my handsome son on the other side never wavered. He continued the signs.

Once, I came home and found the bathroom door locked, from the inside out. No window open you had to be in the bathroom to lock the door!

Another evening, I remember weeping, sobbing, sitting alone… and I got stuck in what I now call a grief tunnel.

The same words echoed in my mind, and out of my mouth, over and over, "Devyne, please let me hear from you."

My mind felt numb as I repeated those words and my body felt pain.

Heaviness.

Death.

Like it was dying.

My heart felt devastation.

Doom.

Like the world was ending.

I'm not sure how long I stayed like that, it must have been several hours.

Trapped.

Even the tears were stuck in place, not dripping, not flowing, just a continuous wetness on my face.

All of me frozen.

A loop of hell.

Then my phone rang. Loud. Louder than it had ever rung before. With a different tone and rhythm. An upward ring, then a downward one. It changed rhythm, tone, and volume.

It was an *unallocated* call. Not spam. No number showed on the screen.

It jolted me out of that loop like I'd been hit with an electric cattle prod.

I answered. I have no idea why.

But it felt like a blessing, like I'd just been released from prison.

I picked up, crying, my voice shaking.

The line was silent.

Then: static. Loud static. Beeping. More static. Gargled, muffled noises.

My body went into shock, half in awe of a miracle, and half in fear.

The religious ideas kicked in. Demons. Hellfire. Every horror movie I could never watch all the way through. Every imagined scene of a clawed hand reaching through the phone… or Freddy Krueger cutting the line and breaking through the window. Yes, I was a product of the '80s. A culture that fears death. That fears life after death. That fears condemnation, judgment, and being sent to hell.

I threw the phone across the room and sat frozen in fear.

But…there was a flicker of something else. A spark. A hidden part of me that whispered, "Did Devyne just call me… from death?"

Over the next week, I received several more calls with the same unusual ringtone and "number unavailable" display.

But I didn't answer.

Out of fear. Out of disbelief. Out of worry that I'd officially gone batshit crazy and lost my grip on reality.

And this would become a theme in the months to follow, Devyne performing miracles from the other side… And me rejecting them, because I couldn't trust myself.

But here's the thing.

I still have the voicemails. Yes, actual voicemails from Devyne, calling from what I believe was Heaven. Later, my other sons listened to them. One of them pointed out something I hadn't fully caught.

There's a part, clear as day, where you can hear, **"I love you, Mom."**

The calls came from an unallocated number. Not disconnected. Not out of service. Unallocated. Even two years later, if you try calling it back, it still says, unallocated. I've had the same phone number for over fifteen years. Worked the same job. I've never once, before or since, received a call like that. One day, I hope to get those voicemails looked at by a professional. I'm not sure what kind of professional, maybe someone in electronic spirit communication.

What I do know is this, I once got a phone call telling me my son was dead.

And three months later…I got another call, on the same exact phone, with my son telling me he was alive, well… and that he loves me.

The signs didn't bring me peace at first.

Let's just be honest, every damn sign came wrapped in days of agony, doubt, fear, and full-on self-gaslighting.

Was I losing it?

Was this grief?

Was this desperation?

Was I making shit up just to survive?

It didn't matter. Devyne kept coming. He never stopped. And over time, he started getting funnier. Bolder. More like… himself. He was always a bit of a prankster in life. He's still a prankster in death.

Sometimes I'd be driving for twelve hours straight, running from the grief, trying to make sense of life without my son and grandson and I'd feel him in the backseat. Not metaphorically, physically.

Pressure on my back when a cop would be trying to hide from speeders, or a deer would cross the road. Dome lights flicking on and off. Weird car beeping. Static in the speakers. Sometimes even spider-web tingles on my scalp or face or neck, always right after I'd say: "Devyne, is that you?"

He'd answer without answering. Sometimes by making the car swerve slightly or the lights flash, or the dash make noises. And sometimes, he'd just laugh at me.

Like when I'd stub my toe on the edge of the bed and hear his voice crack up, "Ha! That's what you get, MA!" He always called me Ma with this weird sarcastic annunciated drawn out MAAA.

Or the time I had this weird vision of ravens. They were everywhere after he died. Flying alongside the car and circling overhead. One day I said, "Okay Dev, if that's you, land on me. Prove it." Immediately, I got a vision of giant raven's dive bombing me, getting tangled in my hair, wings flapping in my face, smacking the shit out of me. I could hear him laughing in my head like, "You wanted a bird, Ma? You sure??"

That's how it started to change. Not by getting softer, but by getting more real.

The real, raw, unedited truth of what awakening looks like when it's born through grief, rage, fear, and love. Devyne and I have a rhythm, an edge, a dark humor, and you as the reader need to feel that. You need to know that awakening isn't all incense and angel numbers. Sometimes it's ravens trying to rip your hair out while your dead kid laughs his ass off.

But even with all of that, the signs, the humor, the "holy shit, this is actually happening" moments, I still couldn't fully trust it.

The signs came and I still doubted.

The miracles happened and I still thought I was crazy.

I was starting to open, yes, but I was also still terrified.

Still wrecked. Still trying to outrun pain driving from state-to-state, family member to family member, at midnight with a ghost in my backseat.

And yet… something was changing.

I was starting to talk to him out loud. Starting to hear him back. Starting to believe, just a little. And that's when Devyne decided to level up. That's when he started nudging me toward the cruise, Helping Parents Heal and toward something I never expected. Helping Parents Heal's mission is to provide support and resources for bereaved parents to find hope and peace by connecting with their children in spirit and sharing experiences in a safe, non-dogmatic community. It aims to help parents transition from grief to a state of hope, enabling them to discuss spiritual experiences and find comfort through a global network of support groups, resources, and virtual meetings.

**The Cruise**

About eight months after Devyne died, and yes, I still say died, even though he gives me shit about it, I went on a cruise. Not for fun. Not for vacation. I went because I was desperate, and because Devyne kept nudging me.

The cruise was called The Awakened Way with Suzanne Giesemann. I didn't know much about her at the time, just that she was a famous medium and people said she was the real deal. I figured if anyone could help me make sense of what was happening, the signs, the pain, the fucking madness of it all, maybe it was her.

Suzanne's not just any medium. She's a former Navy Commander, has a master's in National Security Affairs, and was the aide to the Chairman of the Joint Chiefs of Staff. She left all of that to become a medium and now she's known all over the world. Her waitlist is five years long and usually closed. But there I was… on a boat with her, trying to keep my soul from completely unraveling.

I was paired with a roommate from Helping Parents Heal. One night, my roommate gave me Reiki, and for the first time since I got that god-awful phone call, I felt… peace. Stillness. Something shifted inside me.

I knew then and there, I need to learn this. I need to give this to other moms.

The cruise was filled with parents, seekers, grievers, all of us trying to connect to someone we loved and for the first time, I didn't feel crazy for talking to my dead son. It was normal. I could breathe again.

I met a mom and dad I instantly attached to like a stray dog. She was the Western North Carolina group leader for Helping Parents Heal. We bonded fast, and I'm still connected with that group to this day.

That cruise gave me my people. My tribe. My anchor.

One day, I was sitting on a balcony with the mom I was a roommate with and said, "Wouldn't it be cool if our kids showed us a whale?" Seconds later, not minutes, a whale popped up right in front of us, tail slapping the water, close enough we nearly got splashed. It was easy to celebrate the sign with someone else who believed and didn't doubt or pick it apart.

But even with all that, the signs, the people, the support, I was still barely hanging on.

There were moments I thought, if I just jumped overboard… at least the pain would stop. I think Suzanne sensed it. She quietly pulled me aside and said, "I'm supposed to give you a reading. Don't tell anyone." So of course I'm putting it in a book. Sorry, Suzanne. The actual reading happened about two weeks later, once I was back home, and it shattered me in the best possible way.

She described Devyne exactly.

She said, "He calls you Maaa," in that same exaggerated tone he always used. She somehow knew I was in Texas, even though my cruise name tag said Oregon. She showed me his walk, arms swinging wide and long, just slightly too long for his frame. I could see him in her body. She spoke of the man I was staying with, Devyne's chosen adopted dad, who he had met many years ago in church. He had helped us through a church outreach program. Devyne had bonded with him and kept in touch all these years. He had asked me to come stay with him so he could help take care of Devyne's mom, out of friendship and love for Devyne. He also spent so much money trying to help me get custody of my grandson so that he could stay in his life and fulfill an obligation. He promised Devyne he would take care of his family if anything were to happen.

Devyne told her about their relationship the brotherly/ fatherly love they had and he profusely thanked him for taking care of me. He showed Suzanne that there were straps under my arms and that he was holding me up which was very true and accurate.

She told me he saw the coffee I spilled that morning because I was so nervous about the reading. She knew I'd eaten pizza the night before. She told me he knew about the grief. My grandson. The custody. The courtroom. The nightmare I was living.

He said he understood. That I didn't fail. That I was still trying, just in another state, just in another way. He told her about my Bankruptcy from the legal fees and in fact, she later returned my money.

He talked about forgiveness. Forgiveness for his murder. Forgiveness for losing my grandson. Forgiveness for myself.

That reading gave me something I hadn't felt in months, Proof.

Proof my son still existed. Proof he was still Devyne. Proof he knew me, saw me, loved me and that was the beginning of the real shift.

Suzanne became someone I stayed connected to. She was the first person who validated that what I was experiencing, what I was hearing, writing, and feeling was real. That I wasn't just grief-writing or imagining it. She validated my first experiences of channeled automatic writing with Devyne. Which is a huge piece of Devyne and I's story, our communication, the undeniable proof he communicates.

That's where the next part of the story begins.

---

## Q&A with Suzanne Giesemann

Nearly two years after our first reading, I reached out to Suzanne with some of the questions I had been holding in my heart. I was beyond grateful when she took the time to answer, and even more touched when she gave me permission to include her responses in this book, exactly as she wrote them. Her insight has been part of what helped me truly begin to trust the connection I have with Devyne.

**Question:** Why do spirits so often emphasize forgiveness for their loved ones?

Especially in cases where their physical lives were ended by someone else, what's really happening on the soul level? Devyne really laid it on that I have to remove the stones from my heart during our reading.

**Suzanne:**

"To my understanding, once we shed these bodies, it's like taking off a blindfold that keeps us from seeing who we really are, souls—direct projections of the one Light of Consciousness. With our re(new)ed awareness of our true nature as shining lights, all the baggage that goes with our human stories no longer holds the same meaning. We see that when we are blinded by our human stories, we do things to ourselves and others that souls would never consider because they know we are all connected."

**Question:** How do mediums connect with spirits who are shy, quiet, or unfamiliar with the process of communication?

Dev was shy in life, and you mentioned he was quiet in the reading.

**Suzanne:**

"The medium simply needs to become as clear of a channel as possible. The best way to do this is to be still, turn up the love and gratitude, and passively receive instead of trying."

**Question:** Why do some spirits linger or stay close for years, while others seem to move on more quickly?

Is this about soul contracts, the living's grief, or something else? I thought I was making stuff up because he was always available and answering me in my head. Now, not as much.

**Suzanne:**

"It could be about the reasons you mentioned or other "unfinished business" with those in the spirit's soul family. Some people talk about spirits "moving on" but if there is a possibility of growth for those here or there, they will make themselves available."

**Question:** For those who are just beginning to receive channeled or automatic writing, what guidance would you offer to help them trust the process and begin to verify that the messages are truly from their loved ones in spirit?

I'd love to include your perspective to help my readers feel more confident as they open to this kind of connection.

**Suzanne:**

"This would take longer than I can write, but basically, it's a process of doing the practice, recognizing that it's very human to trust, and just holding the intention that you are making a real connection. Your heart/soul will tell you it's real. Don't hesitate for spirit to tell you something unexpected or something you don't know."

**Question:** You had mentioned afterwards you Googled the murder, saw the accusations, and said you 100% knew that was not my son, you felt his energy and his innocence. I used to daydream that we could put you on the witness stand. LOL. Do you ever wish you could testify for spirits?

**Suzanne:**

"I don't wish I could testify because I can't always be as certain as I was with your son when it's something as important as this. I've witnessed some top-notch, famous psychics be wrong about missing persons cases, for example, and if we can't be 100% certain, that is a challenge. This is why the evidence is so important to me in mediumship. It helps to validate the presence."

**Question:** I'm still reflecting on our first encounter, on your Awakened Way cruise. I was simply standing in line to get your coin and say hello, and something moved you to say that you were meant to give me a reading, despite your full schedule and waitlist. I've always wondered what nudged you in that moment, was it Devyne directly, or were your guides seeing the bigger picture?

**Suzanne:**

"I don't know who it was, but it was likely a combination of Devyne working with my guides. He knew what you needed, and my guides knew how to get my attention until I could get to know his energy."

**Question:** This one more personal to me. You read Devyne just eight months after he passed. If you were to connect with him now, two years later, do you feel there would be any noticeable difference in his communication? Would he have evolved or changed in a way that would be perceptible from your side of the veil?

**Suzanne:**

He may have evolved, but he was already a good communicator. One thing I know is that he will always be your son, and you will have no trouble recognizing him when you meet!

Sent with much love,

Suzanne

---

**Automatic writing: Devs Gift to me on his birthday**

I need to back up and tell you something I didn't fully realize at the time.

Very early on, even before I knew what "automatic writing" was, I was writing to Devyne. I would scribble little messages to him on receipts, scraps of paper, napkins, the backs of envelopes… anything I could find. I'd tell him about court. About my heartbreak. About how sorry I was. About how much I missed him. I'd beg him to show me signs or tell him I thought I'd felt him that day, even if I wasn't sure.

And sometimes, I would hear what I thought he would say back.

At first, I chalked it up to memory, or imagination. I didn't know he was writing with me. I didn't know that the poems that came out of nowhere, the feelings, the phrases that didn't sound like me, were real messages. They were him.

That realization didn't come all at once. It built slowly. Layer by layer. Message by message.

On December 2nd, 2024, what would have been Devyne's 30th birthday, something massive shifted.

It wasn't a hard day like I expected. I should've felt miserable. It was just weeks before the two-year mark of his passing. But instead of pain, I felt… lifted. Like I was floating. Like something beautiful had cracked through. Devyne gave me a gift on his birthday.

**Automatic Writing – Devyne's 30th Birthday**

(December 2, 2024 – received by Jackie)

I was asked to draw cards out of a different deck, The Pegasus Oracle. By being asked, I mean when I centered myself to shuffle my normal deck, an image of my other deck came into my mind, and I felt I was actually supposed to use that deck.

### THE 1ST CARD — #21 PEGASUS OF THE ECLIPSE

Dev: Ma, look at the lights around the blackened sun. What do you see?

The sun might be black, but the light goes on and on.

Ma, look at the right eye on the side, what does it make you feel?

Side-glancing. And there's more light coming in.

Me: Devyne, does this have to do with the right side of my brain?

Dev: NAH. Just look at the light and the fact it is still coming in the eye, even though it is looking straight ahead and not seeing the light.

It is still there. It is still plentiful. Still coming in.

Just like you, Mom. You look straight ahead. You are upset, thinking the worst.

But the light is still seeping in. That is why WE ask you not to think and ruminate too much. It does not matter.

There is still so much light and love around you, and it gets in!

We know you suffer much with thoughts. But we want to show you there is light coming in, no matter what you're thinking.

So please, Ma, for the love of everything, stop thinking you have to do so much to receive light and joy.

Me: What can I do to get my joy and happiness?

Dev: If you stop asking the questions and hush, you will know it's already there. Many times, you ask for answers, but there are none. It simply exists. You simply acknowledge and allow what is already there. Breathe it in.

Me: Thank you, Dev. Any more from this card?

Dev: Read the meaning. It aligns.

ALL IS WELL.


DEV CARD — #27 PEGASUS OF VEGA

Me: What do you want me to see?

Dev: Mom, I am ascending, and your soul is as well.

Look at his tail. Again, in this card, he is looking forward and kind of angry because he cannot see all the light and the beautiful glow that is hitting his heinie.

That light and glow is pushing him, but his face doesn't see it.

Me: Dev, were you mad after you died?

Dev: YES. A little. It took time for me to understand where I am.

But this is more for you, to see how much light and stars you come from.

Even though the front looks angry, you have the universe and all its wonder behind you, pushing you.

No one in this life is trying to harm you, but Ma, the universe is SO SO SO much more than you can know.

We want you to rest easy.

We want you to stop trying so hard.

Yes, we know you don't think you're trying, but you squeeze your eyes so tight.

You think so much about everything.

Ma — ANY CHOICE YOU MAKE IS OKAY.

You spend so much time thinking about this soul's purpose.

LISTEN TO ME.

Everything you do in life is your soul's purpose.

Seriously, stop asking and wondering. Just live!

You can't get it wrong.

Me: Dev, that's from a spiritual point of view. Remember I'm in a human life.

I want to do well and be comfortable.

Your thoughts are making me uncomfortable.


DEV CARD — #12 (BLACK PEGASUS)

Me: What message?

Dev: Ma, it's a she. And not angry, just wise beyond belief.

She is you, Mom. Wise Mom.

You are wise. You know all. You feel all. You are all.

We want you to carry the knowledge you have.

You have experienced all. You are all.

Me: Dev, this sounds like my ego.

Dev: Nope, Ma. This is heavy truth.

And we feel you are now able to understand.

Me: Devyne, are we all God?

Dev: YEP. In a sense.

But I see you imagine the sun and sun rays, or the disco ball and the lights, but that's not exactly it.

It's that you are a thought of God.

Not a physical, just God having a thought.

Me: Yes, but I am me also. My soul is sort of separate-ish?

Dev: NO, MOM.

You are truly experiencing the thought of God.

Me: Then why do I feel like God's having crappy thoughts of me? LOL.

Do I have to change my moods and thoughts to experience a better life?

Dev: YES, MOM.

That is God having a thought that God should change its thoughts so you experience a better life.

Me: Dev, this makes me feel a little sad, like there is no purpose.

Dev: Ma, in a way, that is the point.

But not in a sad way.

In a way that makes you free.

Free to live in this dream as God's thoughts.

Me: What about free will?

Dev: YES, MA. GOD THINKS ABOUT FREE WILL.

Me: Devyne, this is heavy and confusing.

Dev: NO, IT'S NOT.

Make your angry face as you go through this time and space,

but there still is a glow of everything behind you, pushing you.

No matter what angry face you are making, or scowl, or mood

there is still massive light coming in.

IT DOESN'T MATTER WHAT MOOD OR FACE YOU HAVE.

IT DOES NOT CHANGE YOU, your mood, your anything.

Me: Thank you, Devyne. You are awesome. I love you.

Please visit in a human way and don't forget your mom is still Human AF.

———

I didn't expect that day to feel so full of joy.

I didn't expect to laugh, or feel lifted, or feel like I was somehow flying through the veil, hand in hand with my son. But that's what happened.

This wasn't "just" writing.

It was energetic. It was emotional. It was a healing transmission.

It was the first time I fully allowed myself to accept that this was real. That Devyne hadn't left. That he wasn't just dropping feathers and making lights blink. He was co-writing my healing with me.

You don't need to understand every word of Devyne's message to feel what's here.

Let your heart listen. Let your own loved ones speak through the quiet parts of your soul.

Some truths don't come through teaching.

They come through resonance.

Let yourself feel what you need and let the rest float by.

That's what love does.

## The Conversation Continues

That birthday writing was just one of many.

What began as letters to my son, scribbled on napkins, the backs of receipts, torn envelopes, or court documents, slowly became full conversations. At first, I thought I was just imagining what he might say back. But over time, the tone changed. The energy changed. And the words began to come through with a clarity and wisdom that didn't feel like mine alone.

Eventually, I realized something big, we were writing together. Automatic writing for me isn't Devyne moving the pen. I hold the pen, and I hear him his voice sometimes, but it feels more like a thought. But not my thought. I will try to think a thought and his thought will come in so much faster, and literally just drop in my mind and push through my thoughts. When I wrote with him the handwriting would change. I would change I would feel less like myself more like Devyne. More logical and more loved than I could ever love myself. I would feel whole and cherished. But Devyne remained Devyne, his words were sometimes blunt and very direct, no-nonsense. But it didn't come with the feeling of judgment or self-criticism. He would tell me to live again and to love myself. He would tell me to forgive them. He would tell me he understood me, my childhood, my pain, my struggles, and to release myself loathing. He would tell me with the pen writing so hard on the page, it would rip the page. He was emphatic and determined to help me.

**Another Message from Devyne**

This poem came to me from Devyne, clear, rhythmic, emotional, and unlike anything I could have written on my own. It was one of the earliest moments I truly felt him with me, not just in signs or sensations, but in words. They poured through me in a way I can only describe as sacred.

I include it here, because it was a turning point for me, a moment when I stopped asking if he was gone and started learning how to feel him differently. It's raw. It's layered in grief. And it's full of love that never ends.

I hope, as you read it, you feel your own loved one a little closer too.

### *Where Is My Son*

*The lifeless hand of my son I held,*

*He cannot be gone, my broken heart yelled.*

*His beautiful life taken from me,*

*Where is my son—where can he be?*

*I cannot see my son or his breath that once contained life.*

*How could this cold lifeless hand be what once contained my world and sustained such a vibrant man?*

*I am told this is your death, this is the end, now there is no way for this mother's heart to mend.*

*Should I close my eyes and join you in eternal rest?*

*Nothing more for this mother to do, I want to join you in death as your guest.*

*A barely visible flame of hope beckoning me to seek and look, calling me to open life's ever-changing book.*

*A whisper so faint I can barely hear: "Look for your son, for he may be near."*

*My mind's been crying in pain for so long, look where? Where has my son gone?*

*The voice taunts me, "Look through the dark but not with your eyes.*

*Where is my son, is death his disguise?*

*Look with your soul and drown out your grief.*

*I'm showing you signs that bring sweet relief."*

*But where is my son?*

*I must hurry and find him before my mind comes undone.*

*Look up and allow your vision to be burned by the sun.*

*Open your heart and ask again, "Where is my son?"*

*"Look, Mom—look again!*

*I am here in every drop of rain, buried beneath all your pain.*

*Look into the stars. Look at the light shining beneath all your scars.*

*Look for me in the trees, beneath the deep roots, look, Mom, you can see more than the earth's soil and core.*

*Underneath that, there's love, that is me.*

*I am in every boom the cosmos makes.*

*I'm even the vibration and the sound when your heart breaks.*

*I am in the air with birds that fly free.*

*Look, Mom! Look, Mom, it's really me.*

*Hear my songs so beautiful and true.*

*Feel the words I impress upon you.*

*LOOK upon the wondrous skies.*

*Look, Mom, look with more than just your eyes.*

*Open the vastness of your heart.*

*Look deeper past the dark."*

*But I can't, my eyes are shut tight, and I still mourn.*

*My son, your life is gone, and my soul is torn.*

*All of earth feels wrong.*

*I can't find him, for he is gone.*

*The small voice echoes, "Look, Mom, look for your son.*

*You can find me in the glare of the stars that shine with the moon, in the tides that continuously flow every afternoon.*

*Mom, look for me in all that is beyond.*

*Mom, hear my voice, it is clear.*

*Mom, look for me everywhere, and I will always be near.*

*Mom, stop searching and wondering, 'Where is your son?'*

*Feel with the mysterious space of your heart and know I am here.*

*You're always my mother, and your love has won.*

*Be still in your knowing, I am forever your son.*

*I am with you day and night.*

*She took my breath, but she didn't take my light."*

Devyne began nudging me to post the writings. Not to prove anything. Not for attention. But because there were other grieving moms, other broken hearts, other souls searching for the kind of hope and connection we were slowly building. He wanted them to see, your person is still here. They didn't die. Love didn't end. And you can talk to them, most important they can talk to you.

That's how my website was born: www.wespeak2u.com

I didn't come up with that name. He did. I argued with him about it (like I always do), but he won. It's his site. It's where I tell our stories. It's where I post the channeled writings that come through. His words of wisdom and the teachings he so generously gives. It's where I show up for him, and for anyone who needs a thread of connection when everything else feels lost.

There are so many automatic writings I wish I could include in this book. Some are short, some long. Some are funny. Some cosmic. Some are like a punch in the gut and a kiss on the cheek at the same time. Some are so simple it's like a hug spilled onto the page. But each one mattered. Each one changed me. And I've seen how they're beginning to change others, too.

And now, in the most full-circle moment I could never have planned, as I sit here typing this very chapter, I have just finished teaching an automatic writing class for my Western North Carolina Helping Parents Heal group. The very group I found on that cruise. The group that helped me begin to believe. Many moms were able to connect to their children in that class, so much healing happened, and I can see Devyne standing up right with his superman suit cape flowing, so proud of me and the moms!

Devyne isn't just asking me to share our conversations. The writings continue and beautiful beings come in with Devyne to share their loving words and energy with me and other grieving people. There words are wrapped in love and filled with truth there is no death! Love never dies.

This is what happens when you allow grief to become a bridge instead of a wall. When you stop needing permission to believe in the invisible. When you let love find you however it wants to, even through a pen.

# 4

## THE HEALING PATH

After that first Reiki session on the cruise, the one that changed everything, I couldn't stop thinking about it. Something had shifted in me. It was subtle, but deep. I knew I needed more, not just to receive Reiki but to learn it. I needed to be able to offer this kind of healing to others, the way it had been offered to me.

That first session was in August. By November, I found a beautiful, trusted Reiki Master, someone who felt right. She wasn't a stranger. I'd actually met her years earlier on one of my therapist's "retreats" (which were really just intense, emotional deep dives dressed up with a nice name). Back then, I had no idea our paths would cross again like this. But when I found out she was a Reiki Master, something in me just knew she was the one I would learn from.

She was five hours across Texas, a long drive, especially with grief riding shotgun. Devyne hadn't even been gone a year. I was raw. I mean really raw. But I felt safe with her. And at that point in my life, that mattered more than anything.

When it came time for my Level I attunement, I was equal parts excited and scared. I didn't know what to expect. I wasn't sure if Reiki would even work on me. I mean, I was a recovering alcoholic. A sinner, according to some. I had so much shame still tangled up in my spirit. I kept mixing up spirituality with religion, all that old programming still had its claws in me. I wondered if I was doing something wrong, or if I even deserved this kind of healing. But underneath all of that noise, there was a pull I couldn't ignore. A calling I couldn't explain away or scare myself out of.

I didn't walk into Reiki feeling whole. I walked in broken, grieving, confused, and still, something in me knew this was the way forward.

I showed up. That's the truth of it. I showed up for Devyne, even though I was still doubting. Still in pain. Still wondering if any of this would really work.

My teacher, my Reiki Master, had over thirty-five years of experience. She was doing Reiki back when it wasn't trendy, when people thought energy healing was "woo-woo" or strange. She had stayed the course, quietly and powerfully, for decades. And I felt that. Her energy was gentle, loving, and deeply kind.

She had a confidence I didn't. I gulped it up. It balanced the wobble inside me. I genuinely loved her for that. She set me at ease, not with fancy words or some mystical air, but by normalizing Reiki. She didn't make it feel like something only the holy or perfect got to do. She reminded me it was available to anyone who answered the call.

She comforted me. She helped me. And she attuned me to Reiki Level I.

I don't know if the change happened right away, I really don't. But I know this: I felt secure in that attunement. So secure that I immediately started using Reiki on myself, on plants, on my little dog. I didn't have anyone physically around who wanted to receive it, but honestly, Level I is really about self-healing. It's about clearing your own channel first. And I took that seriously.

Suddenly, I was using words I used to make fun of, chakra balancing, energy healing, spiritual cleansing. But it was real now. I had received it. And I was doing my best to understand it.

In the beginning, I struggled. I questioned everything. I constantly felt like I was making it all up, or like I was going crazy. Honestly, that theme ran through my whole spiritual awakening. But I kept going. I kept following the pull. And after what felt like millions of questions and three solid months of practicing and doubting and trusting and circling back, I knew I was ready.

I was ready for Level II.

That meant getting back in the car for another five-hour drive. Money was tight, so I had to save up for it. But I was determined. Because Level II meant something big. I was about to receive the Reiki symbols. I was about to meet my Reiki guide.

**The Symbols**

In Level II Reiki, you receive three sacred symbols. Each one carries its own vibration, its own purpose, and its own key to the unseen.

- **Cho Ku Rei** (pronounced: *choh koo ray*) — The Power Symbol. It amplifies the energy. I call this one the light switch. It turns Reiki "on" and focuses it. It protects, clears, and strengthens. I could feel it humming in my palms.
- **Sei He Ki** (pronounced: *say hay key*) — The Emotional/Mental Symbol. This one cracked me open. It works with trauma, mental patterns, emotional release. When I use it, I often feel waves — like something unbinding inside. It brought up so much and helped me move through it.
- **Hon Sha Ze Sho Nen** (pronounced: *hone shah zay show nen*) — The Distance Symbol. Time and space? This symbol says those are illusions. I could send healing to my past, to Devyne, to people miles away.

It blew my mind and expanded what I thought was impossible.

When my teacher gave me the symbols, something sacred clicked into place. It felt like a reunion. I spent hours drawing those symbols saying their names over and over, not like I was learning something new, but like I was remembering something old.

The Level II attunement was sacred. I embraced every moment of it, not just as a student, but as a mother, a seeker, and a soul in the middle of becoming.

During that attunement, I was guided to my personal Reiki guide, and he appeared to me in full clarity. I saw him. I communicated with him. It wasn't vague or imagined, it was real. I won't go into too much detail, because he feels deeply personal and sacred to me, but within a month, I received full confirmation that he was with me. No question. No doubt.

And then there was the Distance Symbol, Hon Sha Ze Sho Nen.

This meant freedom. This meant healing beyond the physical. This meant helping other grieving moms, even if they weren't in the room. This symbol opened my heart in the best way. It gave me permission to serve, to reach, to extend love across time and space.

I embraced it fully. Scared? Yes. Confused? Totally. Intimidated? Of course.

But I was in. Completely in.

I began working on other mothers who had lost children, people who, like me, were just trying to survive the impossible. And the feedback was incredible. Reiki was working. It was helping. It was easing pain, opening hearts, creating space for light to come in.

And the most wonderfully weird part? I started seeing things. Hearing things.

Passed loved ones began showing up in sessions, and not just for my clients. Devyne started showing up, too. He would talk to me, guide me, support me while I worked on someone else. Sometimes it was subtle, a nudge, a wave of emotion. Other times, it was direct. Words. Images. Clear-as-day messages. I always know when Devyne is going to assist in a Reiki session, he shows me an image where he has his hard hat on, and his work uniform on with his bright orange safety vest and his thick heavy work boots. He has brought in many of the moms' children with him and the beauty of connection. That's healing that's love that's the power of Reiki.

Reiki didn't just open my hands, it opened my intuition.

At first, it was confusing. I didn't understand the symbols I was seeing, or why certain things would show up during a session. But the more I practiced, the more I listened, the clearer it got. Session by session, my confidence grew. My intuitive nudges became more grounded.

And that Distance Symbol, I used it. Holy shit, did I use it.

I used it to send healing to the past, to the relationship Devyne and I had. I used it to send Reiki directly to Devyne in spirit form. I truly believe it strengthened our bond, our communication, our ability to connect across the veil.

I sent Reiki to the courtroom where I had to face the woman who murdered my son.

I sent Reiki to the day I had to let go of custody of my grandson. I send him reiki now wherever he is!

I sent Reiki to the darkest places inside me, the ones that still flinched when light came near. I found during a self-reiki session the massive amount of religious fear and entanglement I had in my body. I wasn't just afraid of Hell I was afraid of God. The God I was taught the jealous punishing God. The God that took away your children and your animals if you disobeyed him. What I found was my creator, my loving God and Jesus, who do not judge, who do not condemn, who unconditionally love you. Who want you to accept every aspect of you to forgive it and to heal it. Who celebrates and jumps for joy every time you show self-love and self-forgiveness. I thank Reiki every day for this gift.

It did a tremendous amount of healing, not just for me, but for the people I was working with. I didn't just believe in it… I lived it.

I spent about a year with my Level II, using it, loving it, and giving away as many Reiki sessions as I possibly could. I was on fire with it. But I never intended to go any further.

Becoming a Reiki Master, that felt out of reach, like it belonged to people who were more pure, more peaceful, more "spiritual" than me.

I cussed. I didn't always eat clean. I still got angry, really angry, about losing my son and my grandson. I battled with my weight. I doubted myself all the time. I just didn't feel like I fit into that polished, peaceful Reiki Master category.

But everything changed with a plane ticket.

I'd been invited to visit the moms in my support group in North Carolina. And suddenly, it hit me: if I became a Reiki Master and Teacher, I wouldn't just be able to give them a session, I could attune them. I could give them the gift of Reiki for themselves. That was it, that was the motivator. That was the leap.

So back in the car I went, another five-hour drive across Texas. But this time, a more confident version of me was behind the wheel. Honestly, it was the feedback that really pushed me forward.

One mom told me, "Jackie, I don't know what you're doing… but it feels like more than Reiki."

Another client could feel every single thing I did during our session. Several grieving moms said they connected directly with their children during the energy work.

Messages started pouring in from complete strangers, telling me how much it helped them.

I was even giving Reiki to people's pets and farm animals from a distance.

Every time I thought, *You're not spiritual enough,* or *You're not worthy,* Devyne would show up and say, "Ma, you just be YOU."

So, I did.

Becoming a Reiki Master was a whole different level of intensity. That attunement, It was sacred. It was alive.

So many beautiful beings showed up. My Reiki Master, with over thirty-five years of experience told me, "Jackie, you've got a full house." I could feel it. The room was full of presence. The energy was electric.

I had already begun sensing Archangel Raphael in my healing sessions, though I wasn't sure if it was really him. I mean an Archangel? That felt way above my pay grade.

Honestly, I kind of expected Jesus to show up. I had heard that some people got guides like Jesus or Archangels when they became Reiki Masters, and a part of me thought, *maybe this will be the moment.*

Maybe I'll get some big sign, something holy and shining, and finally feel like I belong. But me?

I got Rowdy Roddy Piper.

Yes, the WWE wrestler. Full wrestling gear. Kilt and all.

Blowing a horn of victory like it was the most normal thing in the world.

At first, I was like, *What the actual hell is happening right now?* I hadn't thought about him in decades. I hadn't watched wrestling in over twenty years. But there he was, clear as day. Bold. Joyful. Strong. And loud.

I can't say for sure if it was really him or just how my guide chose to present himself. But what I know is this: he came through, and he's never left. He now shows up in almost every session and blows that horn of victory like a damn spiritual hype man. I love him for it.

That's the thing, my Reiki team didn't show up in robes and halos. They showed up in a way that matched me. Raw, real, and a little wild. Cheerleaders, warriors, protectors, goofballs, and guides.

And yes, sacred chaos.

After my attunement, I sat down to do automatic writing, and it poured out of me, celebration, cheering, high-frequency joy from Devyne, from the new guides, from the energy itself. I was overwhelmed by the love and gratitude. I was buzzing. Lit up. Cracked open.

That night, I couldn't wait to start doing Reiki as a Master. In Reiki, once you're attuned, you can use a surrogate, like a stuffed animal, to stand in for someone's energy when you're sending healing from a distance.

I remember sitting in my sister's guest house in this tiny Texas town, hands over my stuffed bunny rabbit, giving Reiki to a complete stranger online, and looking up like, *Oh my God... you must be crazy.*

Even after sixteen months of healing work, spiritual growth, and dozens of powerful sessions, I still had my moments. I still questioned myself. I still didn't feel "enlightened enough."

But here's the truth I came to lean on:

We don't do the healing.

Reiki does the healing. Higher beings, Source, the Universe, God, the Creator, Jesus, Spirit, whatever name you use, that's who does the healing. We're just the channel. The vessel. The hands. Reiki can do no harm and that's what I lean into. That's what comforts me. That's how healing happens.

---

I want to share an experience I had with Archangel Raphael and why I believe in him with my whole heart.

After my Reiki Master attunement, even with all the joy and celebration, there was still this lingering thread of doubt. I kept asking myself, *Was that really Archangel Raphael I've been sensing in my sessions? Or am I just hoping it's him?*

That night, I decided to meditate and call him in, for real.

I had felt his energy before during Reiki sessions with clients. It was subtle but powerful, and there was always this feeling of deep emerald green healing and gentle authority. But I wanted to be sure. I wanted to know how his energy really felt so I could recognize it clearly. So I could feel confident saying, "Yes, Archangel Raphael is here."

So I asked him:

"Please come in. Please show me what your energy feels like so I can know you, recognize you, and trust you're with me when I'm working with others."

And holy moly, did he come in.

I won't lie. I was scared. Not because it felt negative, but because it was so powerful. It was like a thunderstorm of divine energy moving straight through me. I felt this massive, thunderous presence enter the room, and then a lightning bolt of energy went directly through the top of my head and into my heart.

It literally raised me off the bed.

I was frightened. I started apologizing out loud: "I'm so sorry I'm scared! I'm sorry, I don't mean to be!"

Tears rolled down my face. I was overwhelmed. The energy began to gently release… and then, just as I started to settle, it built again, lifting me off the bed again with another wave of divine power. And then… release.

I didn't see him with my eyes, but there was no denying his presence. I felt him, fully, completely, unmistakably. And when it was over, I sank into a peace I can't even describe with human words. I felt like I was the most perfect being on earth. Like there was nothing wrong with me and there never had been. I felt whole. Complete. Blissed out in the most sacred way.

I poured my heart out, weeping, unable to stop thanking him, "Thank you, thank you, I love you, I know you, and you know me."

From that night on, I have never doubted that I am supported by Archangels, angels, and higher beings in my Reiki sessions.

Archangel Raphael has visited me a few more times since then. But now, I'm a little more cautious, I ask him, and the other Archangels, to only show me a little of their energy. Because trust me… even a little goes a long way.

**North Carolina**

Imagine me, a grieving, doubting, still-broken-feeling mother, about to go teach and attune others to Reiki. I wasn't showing up as some polished teacher in flowing robes with a bell and a crystal wand. I was showing up raw and real with a trembling heart and unsteady hands, just hoping to be of service, praying I wouldn't collapse beneath the weight of everything I was carrying.

I stayed with one of my dearest friends, a mother whose story ran almost parallel to mine. She had lost her son to murder too, at the hands of his ex-girlfriend, just six months and one day after I lost Devyne.

Our bond is beyond words. It's like the universe braided our souls together through the fire of grief. We understood each other in a way no one else could, the pain, the betrayal, the nightmare of the court system, the trials, the spiritual awakening that came screaming in whether we were ready for it or not.

We spent almost a week together. We loved on our boys because yes, they were still our boys. We talked about them, about who they were and what they loved. We shared our signs, our messages, our visits, and how it felt to hear them again in the silence. We laughed through the pain. We cried through the joy. We understood.

It felt like we were the only two mothers on Earth who could look each other in the eye and say, "I know. I really, really know."

That week was filled with late-night talks, spiritual downloads, and the deepest kind of soul sisterhood. But it was also the beginning of a new chapter. I wasn't just there to grieve, I was there to give. To attune. To pass on this sacred tool that had changed my life.

The sacredness of attuning those three mothers, women I had previously only been able to offer Reiki sessions to, filled my heart and my entire being with purpose, love, and complete adoration for the process. But more than anything, I was in awe of our strength and the way our children always show up for us.

One of the moms I attuned was Kelley Worth, a radiant soul who had become a lighthouse for grieving mothers. Kelley was the leader of the North Carolina support group, and she was also the mom I'd followed around like a little puppy on The Awakened Way Alaska cruise with Suzanne Giesemann.

She had a beautiful, welcoming space where she did therapy sessions, art therapy, and spiritual work. It was sacred ground, and I was honored beyond words to attune her there. Alongside her was another beloved mom I had also worked with and grown close to, a woman with deep strength and a heart wide open to healing.

That attunement ceremony was magical.

I was absolutely supported and guided by my spirit team and by all of our children in spirit. You could feel them with us, love and healing saturated the space, unmistakable and alive.

After the attunement, Kelley and I participated in a sound healing ceremony together, and that's when it became undeniable, her daughter and Devyne were both with us. Their presence came through so clearly. They were totally with us.

I saw Devyne in my mind, full-body form. I usually only catch glimpses an outline or a brief glance at facial features. I heard his voice, not mine carrying his words. That moment blessed me and wrapped me in pure love and a firmness in my belief. It helped me open in a whole new way. Kelley had the same experience with her daughter. We were in two worlds at once, mothers and children, spirit and living breath.

I'm beyond grateful that I had the opportunity to give back to Kelley, who had given so much to so many others. She was a force of light for grieving mothers, holding space, offering support, pouring herself into service and just a few months after that visit, our beautiful Kelley passed on to be with her daughter.

Her reunion is the sweetest thing our hearts could imagine, but for those of us still here, her absence leaves a deep, aching void. She is missed so much, especially by her husband and the community she held up with such grace and devotion.

The second mom I attuned, one of our fiercest "momma bears," as we call ourselves, brought her own power to the process. She's used her Reiki beautifully, not just for herself or her animals, but to go out into the world and send healing to places devastated by hurricanes and floods across her beloved North Carolina. Her connection to her son on the other side has only deepened since then. Seeing her use Reiki as a force of service and connection fills my heart with so much joy.

And then there was my dear friend, the one who welcomed me into her home for the week. We chose to do her attunement privately, in the comfort of her living room. Just the two of us. It was deeply personal, full of emotion, and perfect in its quiet power. I'm so grateful for that shared moment between two mothers, bonded by loss, and now, by light.

Reiki has given me so much. It's given me healing. Connection. Purpose. Community. Spirit. It's given me tools to hold space, to survive, to lift others as I keep climbing.

Leaving North Carolina after that week was hard. My soul longed to stay longer, to be with the moms, to sit in that sacred circle of friendship and shared knowing. Even now, I ache for that space and those connections.

But what I carry with me is this: the energy we created together is never really gone.

It lives on, in our hands, in our hearts, and in the bond we share with our children in spirit.

---

## Spiritual YouTube Rabbit Hole

After Devyne died, I did what so many grieving people do:

I went searching.

And by searching, I mean deep dive, obsessive, middle-of-the-night YouTube binges where one video leads to another, and suddenly you're listening to a guy in Bali tell you to never eat meat again or you won't ascend... while another woman is sobbing into the camera saying her dead child only comes through when she eats red meat.

Welcome to spiritual YouTube.

At first, I was hungry for answers. Any answers. But I quickly found myself drowning in them instead. There are millions of videos. Hundreds of teachers. And no one agrees.

One person says, "You must meditate for an hour every morning, sitting upright, back straight, no music, no thoughts."

Another says, "Let it be effortless. Lay down. Let your thoughts come and go. There are no rules."

Then someone else says, "If you're not doing breathwork first, your chakras aren't aligned, and you won't reach the higher realms."

Oh, and don't forget the ones who say if you're grieving too hard, your vibration is too low and your loved ones can't reach you.

Imagine being in the deepest pain of your life and hearing that. It's like being handed a thousand maps when you're already lost and every map says, "This way. But also... maybe not."

I tried it all, I am not saying they don't all have tremendous value but when you're grieving and trying to swim your way through dark murky muddy water it can pull you under and make you feel even more stuck, like you are drowning in darkness.

- Guided meditations.
- Binaural beats.

- Kundalini.
- Sitting in silence until my legs went numb.
- Channelers who speak in accents they didn't have before.
- People who say they died for 5 minutes and came back with all the answers.
- People who swear aliens are behind everything.
- People who swear aliens are demons.
- Twin flame chasers.
- Light language.
- Past life healers.
- Shadow work every day or else you're bypassing.

And through it all, the same scream echoed in my soul: *Where the fuck is my son?!*

I didn't want enlightenment.

I didn't want to become a guru.

I just wanted Dev.

I wanted something, anything, that felt real, that gave me solid ground, that didn't shift with every scroll or contradict the last thing I watched.

The contradictions didn't help. The information overload left me more confused, and honestly, more shattered.

And the thing is, I don't regret searching. I think it has made me more flexible, adaptive, broadened my mind, and expanded me in so many ways.

So I'll say this to you, if you're in the rabbit hole right now, you're not crazy. You're not doing it wrong. You're just broken hearted. Standing in the middle of a spiritual super-store where the check-out clerk is on acid.

---

**Sarah**

I was being dragged through the court system, emotionally gutted by the endless trauma of trial, custody, and legal battles.

And then, another heartbreak.

My little dog passed away. She had been a living connection to my grandson, she was given to him while I had him, and he wasn't allowed to take her. Losing her opened a kind of grief I didn't know I still had. I honestly didn't think I could possibly cry anymore tears! It wasn't just grief for the dead, it was grief for the living. I began to wonder if I was cursed and if I should go live in isolation on a mountain alone so as not to spread my bad luck around.

I was overwhelmed beyond words.

And in that moment of vulnerability, I did something I swore I'd never do, I posted Devyne's photo on a free mediumship reading site.

Not that there is anything wrong with that but because Devyne was very clear that he didn't want me to depend on mediums to hear from him. No info. Just the picture. I waited. Nothing.

Other people were getting read, even those who posted after me. I figured, "Of course. Dev's not showing up. He never wanted to be read by strangers."

And then... Sarah showed up. Sarah entered my life quietly but permanently. She didn't just read Devyne, she knew him, she met him, she heard him! His voice. His humor. His essence. She didn't need any information. She just knew.

The reading felt so real, so pure, so unmistakably him, that I cried again.

Oh, and did I mention? Sarah's also a psychiatrist.

So part of me is convinced Dev was like:

*"Girl, you gotta help my mom. She's about to lose it."*

What I didn't expect was that Sarah wouldn't just be a medium, she'd become one of my closest friends. A cheer-leader. A mirror. A co-witness to my healing. Dev loves her. He still comes through for her regularly. He actually likes hanging out with her (which is saying a lot for Devyne) And honestly, I can't imagine my life without her.

That reading with Sarah changed something.

It was the first time in a while I felt that spiritual chaos settle down. Not because she told me the answer, but because she grounded me. That's when I began to realize, some things were actually working. Not because I read about them or followed a trend, but because they brought real peace, real presence, and opened something true inside me.

## A Letter From Sarah:

*I was first introduced to Devyne on May 23, 2024. Jackie had posted a picture of Devyne in a free mediumship Facebook group where I was an administrator. We had a que of over 450 requests and there he was. A young man standing alone in a room in dress slacks, dress shirt, a tie, holding a bright blue bag and less than thrilled that mom made him take a picture, the caption read, "Thank you for the add, my beautiful son in spirit, any messages?". I scrolled through the hundreds of requests on the page daily and always came back to Devyne. I learned long ago that I truly have no choice in who I read. My clients, both earthbound and in Spirit, choose me and it is always a gift that reveals itself at some point during the read.*

*When I finally gave into the "pull" and committed to the read it was a strange connection. Exceptionally strong, but different. I sat with him for over an hour, was given numerous evidences, even prompted to grab Reese's peanut butter cups from my pantry and eat them until my stomach demanded that I stop. It was such a strong connection but when I closed for the night, it just didn't feel complete. I couldn't put my finger on it, it vibrated at the frequency that I know is Spirit, but the content was first person and earthbound. Was he "reliving" his story for me? Not terribly unusual but a little excessive in this case. I went to bed with the determination that I would sit with him again in the morning. In the middle of the night, I woke up and as I got up to get a drink of water it hit me, LOUD as a clap of thunder, "BROTHER!" I said aloud, "It's your brother! I'll talk with YOU in the morning." But it was still a bit of a mystery because the quality of the read was so incredibly unique. The next morning Devyne and I had a marathon reading, everything flowed as I am accustomed to and throughout the day, after providing Jackie with the read, we continued to connect. Initially I did not include the first night's read but as Jackie was resonating with the morning's read and we were able to have some back and forth dialogue, I got a better sense of where she was emotionally and I went out on a limb and asked if she had another son in spirit or if her son had a close friend in spirt and then I gave her that first read. She immediately identified that it resonated with Devyne's earthbound brother. In 30+ years of formal mediumship readings this was an absolute first. Spirits mention their earthbound loved ones all the time, but this was literally a full read from the thoughts, visual perspective, etc., of an earthbound soul! I didn't even know that was possible. Devyne was worried about his brother and selflessly brought his energy forward, first. Wow! The first gift from Devyne, a truly new and amazing experience. Mediums all read and connect in uniquely individual ways, I am no exception. Some connections are just different and I can feel that, while the read is complete, there is more to be learned and shared. And, frankly, sometimes I just really click with a Spirit and we enjoy each other's company. In these instances, I always let Spirit know that in the future they are welcome to reach out when I am open and working. I've been so lucky to meet many new friends, Spirit side, over the years and I cherish each and every one of them. But Devyne, for some inexplicable but completely magical and entirely natural reason has become a permanent part of my Spirit team. I wonder if it isn't because we achieved something really unique and new that day in May. Did we become part of each other's growth and ascension process? It is a beautiful mystery to me but one I am so very thankful for. I did know after that first read that part of Devyne choosing me was to help Jackie in her journey. As I had the opportunity to do that through continued communication with her, Devyne decided to return the favor and begin actively participating in many of my meditations. I affectionately refer to him as my spiritual doorman. Devyne opens doors, literally and figuratively, that I may be struggling to see or open on my own in my ascension and awakening process. It is remarkable. I have even invited him into a few reads with Spirits who are newly transitioned and still getting the "lay of the land". Devyne has become a permanent fixture, always presenting in any scenario where I call on my Guides and Team for assistance. And Devyne, clever and gracious always, often validates my new theories and awakenings by including them quite precisely in automatic writings with Jackie without her having any prior knowledge and, vice versa. The way that Spirts and Source perfectly orchestrate connections will never cease to amaze me and Dev is quite literally one for the books! A teacher, a partner, a wonderfully quirky, analytical, nerdy, overly serious and at the same time absolutely hilarious, light hearted, and wise representative of the Collective Conscience of the Universe and it is such an honor to walk this journey with him, AND Jackie.*

Sarah Garcia, PsyD
Licensed Clinical Psychologist

---

**When Guided Meditations Saved Me From Myself**

So now, let me tell you what helped, what really helped me feel closer to Dev, to myself, and to the unseen world that was trying to hold me through this.

Asking an ex-alcoholic grieving the loss of her son and grandson to sit in stillness and meditate was like asking a war survivor to find peace in a firework show. It just wasn't going to happen. At least, not at first. I started to explore guided meditations, and surprisingly, I didn't hate them. They gave my mind something to do. A voice to follow. A container to feel safe in. And over time, they worked.

Reiki helped too, it calmed my nervous system just enough to open that quiet inner doorway. Soon, I was having powerful experiences. I was connecting with Devyne in ways I hadn't thought were possible. My consciousness was expanding. It wasn't perfect, it wasn't linear, but it was happening.

There were a few people on YouTube I actually did connect with, people whose voices comforted me and helped me feel safe and grounded. And I believe it was that consistent practice, listening to their meditations, letting myself soften, that eventually helped me learn how to meditate on my own.

Even before Devyne's death, I'd had an interest in Near Death Experiences.

Books like *Many Lives, Many Masters* by Dr. Brian Weiss and *Journey of Souls* by Dr. Michael Newton were lifelines for me. They planted the seed that maybe… just maybe… Devyne wasn't gone. Maybe he had just shifted forms. I went deep into NDE stories.

My favorite by far became the *Next Level Soul* podcast. The host has this beautiful way of blending science and spirituality, asking grounded questions, and letting people be real. It helped my nervous system relax. I wasn't just being asked to "believe." I was being shown. And slowly, I began to believe more deeply that Devyne could still be here, with me.

Then, something unexpected happened.

I became fascinated with past life regression and hypnosis. I wanted to find Devyne, see if we'd shared a lifetime before this one. I wasn't sure I believed in reincarnation, but I was open. Curious. Desperate, even. And what I found… was so much more than I bargained for.

I met Robert Schwartz because I was desperate for answers. I needed to know if my son's murder had been planned before this life, if there was some meaning in it or if I had somehow veered way off my path. Robert was kind enough to respond to my email, and that's when he offered me a Life Between Lives (LBL) session.

Just a few days before that, I had been writing with Devyne. I asked him: "Who is Jesus, really?" Not the Jesus of religion. Not the version buried under dogma. Could I know him outside of all that? Could I have a direct relationship with him? And just like Devyne always does, he answered me.

I heard Jesus.

Not in a dramatic or frightening way, but in a way that felt deeply personal. He came through as loving, compassionate, even a little humorous. There was no judgment. Only light.

Then, within days, Robert sent me an introduction to a man in the UK who had written books and taught directly from his personal communication with Jesus. That man had also connected with a mother in Texas who had lost her son to murder. I, in turn, brought in a dear friend from North Carolina, another grieving mother, and the three of us began to Skype with Brian Longhurst. We comforted each other and learned so much.

Brian held us with such gentleness. He poured out the wisdom and teachings of Jesus in a way that felt real and alive.

Do you see the web?

The connection?

The synchronicities?

They're real. And I thank Devyne for helping me find them.

Robert also offered me a scholarship to do a session, something I'll always be grateful for. I was doubtful going in, but open. Willing to try anything. And what happened during that session changed me.

I saw a past life. I visited that sacred space between lives and I spoke with my guides, with Devyne, and with a council of souls who were helping me understand my journey.

But the moment that knocked the air out of my chest was this, I saw Paige, Devyne's ex-wife, the woman responsible for his death as my child in that past life.

Let that sit for a second.

The woman who murdered my son…was once my daughter. And in that past life, I loved her. Can you imagine what my body went through seeing her that way? Not as a killer. Not as an enemy. But as my child. Through the eyes of a mother.

If I lost you there, I understand.

Honestly, I almost lost myself. It was too much. Too big. Too multidimensional for my human brain to hold. But it wouldn't let me go. That vision changed me. And it changed the way I saw her, especially in the courtroom.

The words kept echoing in my mind, soft and haunting: *What if…?*

But then I began to wonder, what if reincarnation is real? What if I am not a victim, but my soul planned this life before I was even born? What if there's more going on here than I understand? What if we've done this before? What if this pain is part of something bigger?

Looking back now, I realize something even deeper.

While writing this book, I pulled out my old journal and reread what I had seen and heard in that session. It had been over a year. And suddenly, parts of it started to make sense. Things that felt too big, too strange, too overwhelming to hold at the time... started to integrate.

That's the thing no one tells you about this path, some truths don't land right away. Some healings are delayed reactions. Some soul-level wisdom has to drip into your nervous system drop by drop until your body and mind can handle it.

This journey isn't a straight line.

It's spirals. Circles. Backtracks. It is grief mixed with grace and confusion mixed with clarity.

I never stopped learning. I never stopped absorbing all the information, books, YouTube, interviews, regressions, dreams. And while a lot of it overwhelmed me in the beginning, I've learned that not everything is meant to make sense right away.

Sometimes it takes time. Sometimes, you have to live a little more before a teaching can land. Sometimes, the wisdom waits until your heart is soft enough to receive it.

So if you're reading this and thinking, "I don't get it yet," or "I'm not sure I believe in all this," that's okay.

You don't have to make it all make sense right now. Just hold it loosely. Let it move through you. Let it take the time it needs.

---

**The Day Devyne Spoke Through Me**

Somewhere along the way, after all the YouTube confusion and the guided meditations, I started to understand binaural beats. And by understand, I don't mean in a technical, scientific way.

I mean I felt them.

Binaural beats use two tones, one in each ear, that gently guide your brainwaves into different states. It's like giving your nervous system a sound-based invitation to calm down, expand, or tune in. And somehow, it worked for me. The beats helped me soften into that inner space where Devyne could reach me.

To this day, it's still my favorite way to meditate.

Although now, I can also sit in silence, feel into my energy field, and balance and clear my chakras with ease. That didn't happen overnight. But it happened. I opened the door, and Devyne kept showing me how to walk through it.

One of the books that helped me the most was *The Art of Psychic Reiki* by Lisa Campion.

When I first started this journey, I couldn't even finish a book, I was too wrecked, too scattered.

Which is why I've attempted to keep this book short, by the way. I know what deep grief does to a brain.

I bought Lisa's book both as a physical copy and on Audible. I poured over the pages. Finally, something made sense. She helped me understand what I had been going through as an empath for decades. Why I always felt everything. Why I often shut down. Why Reiki had opened me up the way it did. She helped me trust my own psychic abilities.

Yes, I said it.

I have psychic abilities.

I can say that out loud now and I trust that truth.

Lisa's teaching resonated so deeply, I ended up taking her psychic training classes. That was a big deal for me, because I'm skeptical as hell about where I spend my money or who I choose to learn from. But Devyne leaned in. He helped make it happen.

I trusted her. And now, she's part of our team, part of Devyne's circle of support for me. I lean on her often, and she always shows up.

My journey with past life regression wasn't done. Devyne had another miracle lined up.

I found a local QHHT past life regressionist who was still practicing and offered to do a session for free. That was Dev all the way. He was tight with money in life, and apparently, he still watches over my spending in spirit.

That session changed everything.

It happened a few days after the channeled writing I received on Devyne's 30th birthday, the one that felt like it cracked something wide open. I was still riding that wave when I went in for the regression. And what happened next... I still don't have full words for it.

Devyne came into the session and spoke through me.

He used my voice and my body, but it wasn't me speaking, it was him. He joked with the practitioner. He gave her specific, mind-blowing information about the universe and the science of the planets, things I would never have known. He told her that I was psychic, that I was gifted, and that I was supposed to teach others. He verified that Paige had been my daughter in a past life. He was playful, wise, and alive.

The whole thing was recorded, and I sent the session to several people I trust, psychic friends, Mediums I knew and spiritual teachers.

Every single one of them said the same thing:

"That was him. That was Devyne."

Afterward, I was buzzing.

I could barely contain myself, I stayed in a motel in San Antonio that night, just a few hours from where I live. The next morning, I decided to visit the botanical gardens nearby. As I was walking, still in a daze, talking to Devyne in my head, the regressionist called me.

Her voice was light, kind of giddy.

She said, "I just wanted you to know… your son is still here with me. He's making fun of me. He's giving me practical life advice and big answers to big questions." My eyes welled up. Tears of gratitude. For her and for Devyne. For this strange, beautiful life, as broken as it had been.

I tucked my phone away in my purse and continued walking. Still speaking with Devyne in my heart, I asked him, "How is this even possible?," "How are you still here?"

Just then, my phone, buried in my purse, started talking.

Google's voice suddenly said, "Once there lived a protago-nist… and some supporting characters. Together, they went on a journey, and twist ending, it was all a dream."

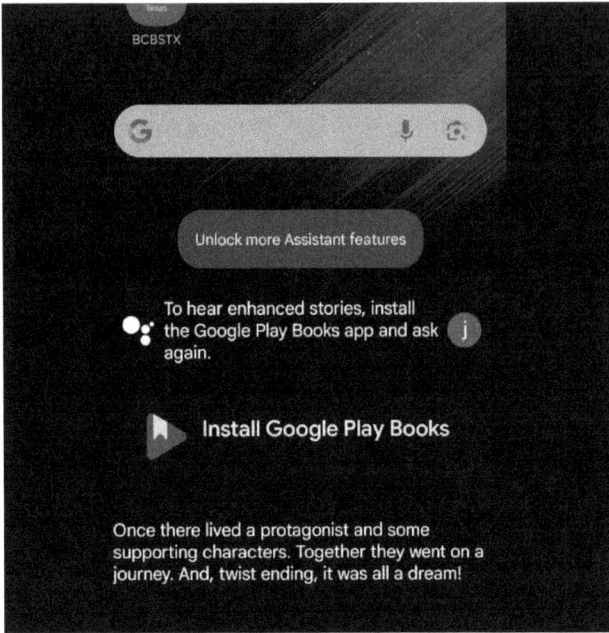

I froze. I pulled out my phone and took a screenshot. No one had touched it. No buttons had been pressed.

It was Devyne, again.

It hasn't stopped. I'm still in contact with the practitioner from that session. She told me recently that Devyne still comes through for her. She calls on him when she's stuck or needs guidance, because his answers are always the best. He helps her and she trusts him. The wildest part is, she now asks me for help too. Because I'm psychic. Because I'm connected. Because Devyne was right. He always knew who I was, even when I didn't. And now… I do too.

### The Gift of Nathan (Straight From Devyne)

Let me be really honest: I've never liked life coaches.

They always felt cringey to me, like one of those Facebook ads that says, "Become a certified coach in 7 days for $7!" No thanks.

With all the work I've done with women over the years, I have never felt drawn to work with men in a healing way. Because of all the past trauma and abuse I had endured at the hands of men, I have never felt safe to work with them when it came to being vulnerable. But just after Devyne came through that first verbal channeling during a past life regression, I started writing to him, asking for help. I told him I needed someone real. Someone I could trust in person. Someone to help me sort through the flood of spiritual downloads, signs, awakenings, and contradictions that were crashing into me daily. I didn't need a guru. I needed an anchor.

That's when Nathan showed up.

Out of nowhere, I got this Facebook message offering five free coaching sessions to help me get clarity, peace, and move forward in life. I wouldn't have touched it with a ten-foot pole, but Devyne was pushing hard.

So I said yes.

Right away, Nathan started saying, "I don't know why, but I'm being led to go outside my structured 5-day program with you. There's something deeper here." He had no idea what he was signing up for.

In one of our early sessions, he led me into a meditation so deep, Devyne came through again. This time, full-on.

Speaking through me to Nathan. He told him exactly what I needed. How to guide me. What the next part of my healing should look like. It was loving, wise, direct and totally undeniable. That was the moment I knew, Nathan wasn't just a coach, he was a gift from Devyne.

Since then, Nathan and I have become true spiritual partners, and friends. We now work together on clients, doing deep spiritual and energetic healing work that's being guided from the other side. Lineage work. Past life clearing. Psychic development. Whatever people need, the guidance shows us. He helps me stay grounded, calm, and clear. Nathan makes me feel safe, seen, and heard in a way I didn't know I needed. He opens the space so gently, never judging, always holding me with patience and clarity. I'd love to say he never pushes, but that's not quite true (and he'd probably laugh reading this). The truth is, he does push, when I need it. He sees what I carry, and he knows I have more to offer, and he believes in me even when I forget how to believe in myself. His patience and kindness help me settle into my gifts instead of running from them.

Thanks to him, and thanks to Devyne for nudging me, I now have structure in my days. I keep a schedule. I hold sessions. I can show up fully for the people I'm meant to help. My life isn't just surviving anymore. It's manageable. It's meaningful. And dare I say beautiful. I think one of the biggest truths I've learned on this journey is, our loved ones on the other side know what we need. They can see things we can't. And they do everything in their power to guide us, bringing the right people, opportunities, and moments into our path.

There is a catch, we still have to say yes. We still have to open the door.

Devyne never asked me not to grieve. He never told me to suck it up or pretend I was okay. But he did ask me not to get stuck. Not to give up. Not to quit living.

And when he brings gifts, like Nathan, or signs, or whispers, or synchronicities, we honor them by paying attention. By opening the door. Even if we're scared. Even if it doesn't make sense at first.

That's how healing starts. That's how the new path unfolds.

And here's the thing I'm still realizing, saying yes to Nathan was really me saying yes to Devyne.

Yes to trusting him.

Yes to the path.

Yes to not just surviving, but living.

My life keeps shifting in ways I never imagined. I'm clearer. Calmer. Stronger. I show up for my clients. I show up for my family. I show up for myself. And every time I say yes to a new nudge, every time I listen, even when I don't understand why, It opens something bigger.

That's the magic of this whole journey.

When we say yes, even scared, even skeptical, we say yes to healing.

We say yes to them. And somehow, they walk with us every step of the way.

---

### Before Devyne "Died" (He Still Argues With That Word)

So, allow me to take you back for a minute. Back to a time when all of my children were still alive, what I call "pre-Devyne's death."

He corrects me every time I say that, by the way, "There's no death, Ma." I know, Dev... but it sure feels like it.

At that point in my life, I had just gone to rehab and gotten sober. It was a powerful experience, as many of us know, getting sober doesn't mean you're instantly healed. I got clean, yes. But I was still carrying decades of trauma, grief, and unprocessed pain. And instead of healing, I did what so many people do, I replaced one addiction with another.

I fell headfirst into a toxic relationship with a man who had even more demons than I did. At first, I thought I was madly in love. But in truth, I had just swapped the bottle for chaos.

I stayed sober for about a year. Then came COVID.

I had just bought my first home. Less than two days later, we had a huge fight. I knew he was lying, cheating, and using drugs and I did what I had always done to cope, I drank. Then I burned some of his things in the bathtub. What I didn't know was that those things would cause a chemical fire and that I would burn down half the house.

With me in it.

I died that night. I was revived, but not before sustaining third-degree burns on 30% of my body. I spent six weeks in the burn unit, went through three skin graft surgeries, and was left physically and emotionally shredded. Not long after that, he went fully off the deep end. There was a manhunt for him, with dogs, helicopters, the works. He's now serving life in prison.

Trying to heal from that, physically, spiritually, emotionally, was one of the hardest things I've ever done. It broke me and it broke Devyne's heart.

He flew to Texas to check on me. He was so angry. But underneath that anger was deep, gutted love. That was the last time I ever took a drink.

In the months surrounding that critical date, September 7, 2020, while trying to make sense of what had happened, I began planting seeds of something new. I didn't know it then, but that fire, the one that nearly took me, was the very thing God would use to light the next part of my path.

**Transforming Tumbleweeds: Turning Pain Into Purpose**

Out of the ashes, literally, I started a women's empowerment nonprofit called **Transforming Tumbleweeds**.

**Our Vision:**

A world where women don't feel alone in their struggles, where they feel empowered, where their voices are heard, and where they are worthy of love and kindness, even from a complete stranger.

**Our Mission:**

To empower women to heal… so they can empower other women.

**Our Purpose:**

To help women understand they don't need someone else to "fix" them, they're not broken. Their stories matter. Their pain matters. They deserve love and respect, no matter what they've been through.

And I'll say this loud and clear:

"If God can use me, a woman who had just come out of rehab, who burned down her house, who'd survived trauma most people don't speak of, He can use anyone."

I am proof.

It is not that people don't fall apart, but that they can be put back together in ways more beautiful than before.

I bring this up because this nonprofit became something Devyne really loved. He supported it in ways I never expected, fundraising, giving me ideas, cheering me on. He believed in it, and he believed in me.

That was a kind of healing I didn't even know I needed.

Before Devyne transitioned, (died, passed, exited the planet, however we want to phrase it), I had the honor of writing a chapter in a co-authored book about my experience with rehab, sobriety, and founding the nonprofit.

I sat down to write it on December 14th, 2022. And the whole thing poured out of me in just a few hours. It wasn't perfect. It was a rough draft. But it was whole. I was proud of it and Devyne was proud of it too.

Then came December 16th, 2022.

The call.

The news.

My world shattered.

Devyne never got to see the chapter polished or published. And truthfully… neither did I. By the time the book launched, I was already in the middle of losing my grandson in court. I couldn't bear to go back to it. But the universe, once again, gave me an angel.

Mary Gooden, the writing coach and publisher of Divine Destiny Publishing, stepped in and made it happen. She edited, organized, lifted, and carried that book forward when I couldn't. It went on to become a best-seller in multiple countries and categories. Mary held me through months of grief, spiritual chaos, and every raw, soul-shaking question I could throw at her. At the time, she was the most spiritual person I knew. Her love and steady presence are part of why I'm even writing this book now. Connect with Mary: www.marygooden.com

It's amazing how people show up when your world falls apart.

Some become lifelines.

Some become family.

I've been blessed with both.

Looking back now, I can say this with my whole heart, "God doesn't waste anything. Not the fire. Not even the heartbreak and definitely not you."

I realize I've thrown so many signs at you. But when I shared my early signs, they were so full of grief and confusion. The joy got muddied in the deep, murky waters of my despair and collided with my beliefs and my unworthiness. So let me share some of the times the signs brought me the peace, the unconditional love, and the utter joy and clarity that they are meant to bring

**The Thanksgiving Pictures**

That first Thanksgiving without Devyne nearly killed me. I was driving five hours to my sister's house, bawling, shaking, not even sure why I was going. I guess I just didn't want to be alone. Somewhere in the middle of that drive, I broke. Not the quiet tears kind of grief, the full-body sobbing, screaming in the car, asking the same questions over and over like a damn lunatic kind of grief.

"Dev, what are you doing?"

"What is your life like now?"

"What do you do all day?"

"Is there even a 'day' and 'night' anymore?"

I must have said it a hundred times.

My phone was facedown where I couldn't even reach it. I wasn't touching it. I wasn't doing anything except crying and begging.

When I got to my sister's, I was tired, I think I fell asleep still asking those questions. The next morning, Thanksgiving Day, I woke up and opened my phone and I saw something that took the air out of my lungs.

Photos. Tons of them.

Pictures I never took. Pictures that weren't there before. The first one?

A man's legs, dangling above the ocean, like he was paragliding. No face. Just legs, feet, water. Freedom.

Then more kept popping up throughout the day. Hands scooping food. Thanksgiving plates being passed. A TV playing the parade with floats going by. No faces. No people. Just the feeling of the holiday, the stuff I thought he'd miss.

It was like he was answering me.

*"Ma… I'm living.*

*I'm free.*

*I'm in the sky.*

*I'm at your table.*

*I'm still here with you.*

*I'm still part of this."*

I told everyone. Even the skeptics in my family. Even the ones who roll their eyes when I say Dev gives me signs. I didn't care. I still don't. I know what I felt. I know what I saw. I know it was him. It's still one of the clearest, most undeniable signs Devyne ever gave me. Of course he did it that way, silent, visual, direct.

Just like him.

On what would have been the second anniversary of Devyne's death, I made a conscious decision, I wasn't going to stay home and spiral. I was still riding the spiritual high from the automatic writing he had given me, and from the powerful verbal channeling that had come through during my past life regression. His message was clear, he didn't want me to grieve endlessly. He wanted me to build on the miracles that had just unfolded.

So I left. I booked a cheap room in Corpus Christi, right on the beach. I told myself I was going for work, but really, I was going to choose life. To step toward healing. To try celebrating myself and my journey instead of staying frozen in the despair of that date.

I got there early and decided to walk down to the beach before check-in. The sun warmed my face, and for a moment, I allowed myself to feel it. To see the beauty again. To remember that life still existed beyond loss.

As I walked, I spotted a large pile of bird feathers up ahead. My heart skipped, could this be a sign from Devyne? A wink from him on his death day? But then I looked up and saw an entire flock of seagulls flying overhead. I laughed out loud, saying, "Oh shit, Devyne, I can't take this as a sign. Look at all these birds!"

Immediately, I heard his voice, clear, confident, and playful:

"Don't worry, Ma. There's a big sign."

I kept walking, just ten more feet, and right in front of me, being battered by the waves, was a Bible. Waterlogged, covered in foam, but somehow completely intact. I felt that familiar "spiderweb" sensation across the top of my head, my face, and neck, that energetic confirmation that told me without a doubt, this was for me. This was from him.

I picked it up, and right there, in big bold letters, it said:

"GOD IS THE ANSWER."

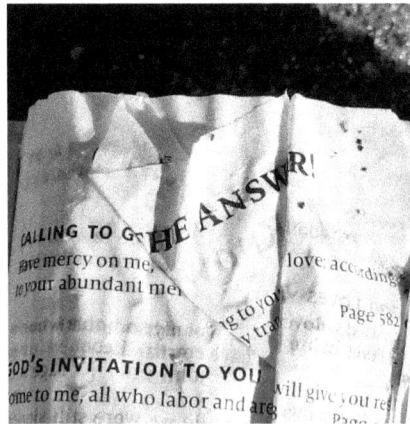

## He Was Reaching All of Us

Some of the most powerful signs I've received didn't come to me at all. They came to the people I love.

I have four sisters, three of whom are half-sisters from both my mom and my dad's previous marriages. My family has been riddled with trauma, addictions, sexual abuse, and violence. My oldest sister from my father's side is quite a bit older than me, and she was my favorite human when I was growing up. I was the same age as her own boys, and I felt more like her daughter than her sister.

Unfortunately, she also experienced the murder of her youngest son and devastation through family courts, trying to have a relationship with his children. She helped me and supported me through all the aftermath of losing my son and then my grandson. I am forever thankful for her wisdom and compassion.

My other sister on my mom's side, who I am very close to, has had a very special on-and-off relationship with me due to my life choices, especially my alcoholism. But through all of my life, she was there in a way no one else ever had been. She married and had a good husband, something I could never attain. She was stable and did a fantastic job raising her children.

When Devyne was a kid, she was his favorite human. He loved being with his aunt. He was so impressed when we went to her house because she was so well organized, socks neatly matched and tucked into drawers, quiet routines, peaceful energy. It was a stark contrast to our house, where homework often felt like a battlefield, food was thrown, and tempers flared. He would spend as much time at her house as he could.

My children also loved and adored her husband, and my younger children often called him "Uncle Dad."

Then, tragedy struck her family, too. When her daughter was barely eighteen, she passed from meningitis. Something that rocked all of our worlds and changed my sister deeply. I could have no idea what she went through until it became my own experience.

But my sister did not believe in an afterlife. She described herself as an atheist, deeply rooted in science. I could never imagine what that must feel like, to lose a child and to think they simply no longer exist.

And then Devyne appeared to her. She called me, completely freaked out. This experience is deeply personal for her, but what she shared is profound: Devyne was there, unmistakably real. He showed her how much he loved me. She kept repeating, "Oh Jackie, he's here, and he loves you so much. He forgives you, and he is so proud of your sobriety and your strength in all that you're doing."

What it meant to me was the whole world. The fact that Devyne reached her, a woman who had never believed in an afterlife and who always kept her composure, it felt like a miracle. The message felt undeniably real, coming through someone so grounded and logical, and it hit me in a way I could never have anticipated. In that moment, I knew without a doubt that he was still here, still loving us, still communicating with us in ways that transcended what I thought was possible.

He was humorous too, going through her sock drawer. And in that moment, as she described it, he ripped the door to heaven open, showing her that heaven is real and that her beautiful daughter still exists. He also expressed concern and asked her to try to protect his son. It was confusing, disorienting, and overwhelming for her, but it changed everything.

We haven't talked about it too much since then, but she listens to my signs and believes Devyne still exists. I love that he did this for both of us.

After Devyne passed, my youngest son Daniel met and married a beautiful woman. She joined our shattered family in the middle of the worst season of our lives, with her little boy, just three years old at the time. Now he's about to start kindergarten. I love them both more than words. Daniel beams when he talks about him. You'd never know they weren't biologically related.

His wife was just beginning her spiritual awakening, and I had the honor of attuning her to Reiki. She's a natural healer, gifted, intuitive, and open. She's also become family in every way that matters.

One night, she gave Daniel Reiki. He went into a partial trance, during the session Devyne had spoken to him and through him. Racheal asked the questions and was able to direct parts of the discussion. I didn't ask for details, that part was between them.

But he did share this:

"Dev said, 'I have toes too… just not like these ones.'"

If you knew Dev, you know that sounds exactly like him.

Daniel's had more moments like that. Dev has written things on Daniels phone. It's changed everything, for both of us. I wasn't the only one hearing him. I wasn't crazy. He was reaching all of us.

Diego, my third child, is the strong, silent type, a true cowboy who works on a sprawling ranch in the Steens Mountains of Eastern Oregon and trains horses for a living. In the months after Devyne passed, he was my rock. He carried so much of the grief quietly, staying steady, shouldering his own pain while also holding me up through mine. He was the backbone I leaned on when the world felt unbearable, and his quiet strength kept us both moving forward.

Then came another heartbreak. Our good horse, Ace, a 16-hand black horse with a massive mane and tail, built to cover forty miles or more a day gathering cattle and mending fences, needed to be rushed four hours away to an emergency vet. I was out of town, completely helpless, and hearing Diego, usually so unshakable, panicked on the other end of the phone shattered me. Ultimately, Diego had to make the gut-wrenching decision to put Ace down. Seeing my son, normally so composed, suddenly vulnerable and tender, brought me to my knees in grief all over again. In the midst of that raw pain, Diego quietly said that he felt better knowing his brother in heaven now had a good horse. That moment, small and unspoken in many ways, was sacred and unforgettable, a reminder that love, connection, and healing can show up even in the darkest, most devastating times

Even his chosen father, his mentor, got a visit. This man is deeply rooted in the Bible, very logical, and extremely skeptical of all the "sign stuff." But on the long drive back from Oregon after the sentencing, when the DA let her plea slide to just twenty years for first-degree manslaughter, he said, "I keep feeling something pushing on my seat. Thought it was the dog, but the dogs aren't near me. I looked back. Sure enough, nowhere near him. I said, "That's what Dev does to me. That's how I know he's with me."

And right then, it happened again. He smiled, a real smile. And when we got home, after thirty hours of driving, he said: "I think I'll sit in the truck a little longer. Just in case Dev wants to push on my back again." That was a moment I'll never forget.

The signs are real. Even if you don't believe. Even if you doubt. Even if you think you're too logical, too broken, too skeptical. They come. Our loved ones don't stop loving us just because they've changed form. They don't need you to believe in magic, they are the magic. And they'll use anything they can to show you they're still here.

So if you've ever felt something… heard something… gotten a message that made no sense but hit you deep in the chest? Please trust it. That's love. That's them. That's real. That's them showing you death is an illusion.

I know I've thrown a lot of sadness, grief, and spiritual confusion your way in these pages. And trust me, I wish I could give you a cleaner, smoother, more graceful version of how I've changed… how I've come to better understand and communicate with Devyne. But the truth is, it was messy. Really messy.

I've spent a lot of time throughout this book showing you the inside of my grief, my confusion, my resistance, my denial. And it wasn't always pretty. But I shared it all because I hope that somewhere in the chaos, you can find something to hold onto. Maybe even something that helps you make sense of your own story.

What I want most is for you to know this, your loved ones are not gone. Your spirit team has never left you even if you were never aware that they existed. Even when you're screaming. Even when you're spiraling. Even when you feel like you can no longer go on. They are still with you. They are still loving you. They are still guiding you. They will use anything, your belief system, your doubt, your heartbreak, your weirdest dreams, to show you that love continues.

You don't need to have it all together to be met by something higher. I didn't. I was raw, tired, barely holding on and still, the signs came. Still, the love found me. If it can reach someone like me in that state, it can reach you too.

I don't believe you have to be in a high vibration to receive signs, comfort, or healing from your loved ones. I know some spiritual teachers say you need to "raise your frequency" to connect, but that's only part of the picture. Sure, you might not have a full-on mediumship conversation when you're in the depths of despair, but your people don't stop showing up. They know your grief is part of your growth. They're not waiting for you to get it all together, they're walking with you through it.

I also want to walk beside you in your grief and your awakening. I want to say the things other people might be afraid to say. I will never pretend to be okay or be someone or somewhere I am not. I want to be living proof that no matter what your past looks like, no matter how chaotic your healing has been, God can still use you. Your loved ones can still guide you. Your soul can still rise.

So if you're here now, wondering how the hell to move forward, I want to offer a few things that have helped me.

Because while I've traveled deep into the spiritual rabbit hole (and yes, it's real), the thing I've learned is that there's not just one right way. We are all so beautifully unique, which means what works for one person might not work for another.

So take what resonates. Leave the rest. There is no single truth.

Our consciousness evolves, and so do our answers.

Devyne tells me we never stop learning, even after death.

## What Actually Helped

If you saw my YouTube, google search, chat, and audible history you would see how difficult it was for me to slim this down for you to take in.

First and foremost, clearing my chakras and my energy field. And if you're like me in the beginning, you're probably thinking, "What the hell is a chakra, and why should I care?"

Let me break it down Jackie-style.

## Chakras & Energy Fields — The No-Nonsense, Slightly Sassier Guide

Your body is like a spiritual Wi-Fi tower. We all believe in an invisible frequency that connects us instantly, even when we are thousands of miles away, that's our Wi-Fi energy field. It's constantly sending and receiving signals, from people, places, spirit guides, grief, chaos, intuition, and yes… your mother-in-law. Your energy field (aka aura) is what picks all that up. It surrounds your body like an invisible mood ring made of vibes. Inside of you, you've got these little spinning power hubs called chakras.

They're like emotional USB ports, and when they're flowing well, your life feels more aligned, more peaceful. But when they're blocked? Oof. You feel it.

Here's the quick breakdown:

Chakra: (Red) Root

Where it's located: Base of spine

What it handles: Safety, security, money

When it's out of whack: You feel anxious, ungrounded, unsafe

Chakra: (Orange) Sacral

Where it's located: Below belly button

What it handles: Emotions, pleasure, creativity

When it's out of whack: You feel numb, blocked, overly sensitive

Chakra: (Yellow) Solar Plexus

Where it's located: Upper stomach

What it handles: Confidence, boundaries, power

When it's out of whack: You feel angry, insecure, powerless

Chakra: (Green) Heart

Where it's located: Center of chest

What it handles: Love, forgiveness, grief

When it's out of whack: You feel shut down, lonely, jealous

Chakra: (Blue) Throat

Where it's located: Throat

What it handles: Truth, expression, communication

When it's out of whack: You feel voiceless or overshare like crazy

Chakra: (Indigo) Third Eye

Where it's located: Forehead

What it handles: Intuition, clarity

When it's out of whack: You feel foggy, disconnected, over-thinking

Chakra: (Violet) Crown

Where it's located: Top of head

What it handles: Connection to spirit, God, Source

When it's out of whack: You feel hopeless, lost, over-it-all

Now, I don't expect you to memorize all this. But if you've been feeling "off," blocked, tired, or like life just keeps swirling… your energy field might need a little tune-up.

## How to Clear That Energy (Without Buying a Crystal Throne)

Here's what's worked for me, a mom, a survivor, a healer who didn't even know she was healer

### 1. Salt Baths
Salt pulls heavy energy out. Water smooths the nervous system it also amplifies your ability to hear and feel spirit your

creator and your loved ones. (Add a good cry and you've basically had a full chakra facial.)

## 2. Reiki
Whether you get it from a practitioner, find a trusted source on you tube or learn it yourself, Reiki is gentle, powerful, and accessible.

## 3. Laugh. Cry. Scream into a pillow.
Your emotions are energy. Let them move.

**4. Movement although I struggle with this still.** My grief and past injuries tend to make me stuck and hard to move. So whatever your able to do, do it! Devyne reminds me this daily.

**5. Nature** I cannot stress this enough any version of nature sunlight coming through your window a house plant if that's all you have the strength to do in those early days.

---

## Try this Waterfall Energy Clearing (for Grief and Early Healing)

Close your eyes for a moment—right here, right now.

Take one slow, deep breath... and then another.

Now imagine this with me:

Above you, a set of vast, loving hands, God's hands, gently open.

From them pours a steady, glowing stream of light.

White. Or golden. Or whatever color your soul needs today.

This is not just light, it's living, intelligent energy.

It knows exactly where you're hurting.

Exactly what you're ready to let go of.

Feel it flowing down over your head,

into your face, your shoulders, your chest.

Down your arms, your back, your belly, your legs…

until it pools gently at your feet and soaks into the earth.

Let this waterfall cleanse you.

Let it carry away the heaviness, the ache, the fog.

You don't have to do anything, just allow.

Grief is not a block. It's not a failure.

It's a passage, and you're still walking through it.

So take another breath.

Let the light stay with you for as long as you need.

And know you can return to this waterfall anytime, even in the real shower.

You are not alone.

You are being held.

---

**My Favorite Tools & Teachers. Tried, Tested, and Truly Helpful**

I know spiritual tools can feel overwhelming, especially when you're deep in grief or just waking up to all of this. So I want to keep this simple. These are the tools, meditations, and voices I trust. I've used them personally, and I often suggest them to my clients, friends, and anyone walking through the fog of loss, confusion, or awakening.

You don't need to do them all, just pick one that resonates. Trust your body. Trust your gut. That's your spirit leading you.

### Automatic Writing Experience (AWE) Class – Michael Sandler

Although I was already automatic writing when I found his class it brought me a lot of confirmation and great new ways to connect.

It became a key part of my healing process and spiritual connection.

Website: https://inspirenationuniversity.com

## Meditation (Especially for Beginners)

### • Suzanne Giesemann – *Sip of the Divine*

Just 3 minutes long. A perfect start for anyone who "can't meditate." She blends presence with peace. Great for busy minds and heavy hearts.

## For Chakra Clearing & Energy Healing

### • Reiki Rachael – 10-Minute Chakra Cleanse

Reiki-infused, gentle, and effective. Not too long or overwhelming. Perfect to do before sleep or in the morning to reset. Reiki Rachael – is a wonderful channel to guide reiki sessions on:

- Binaural Beats for Deep Healing
- Grief & Nervous System Repair

Look for titles like EMDR + Binaural Beats for Grief, Anxiety, or PTSD. These help regulate your nervous system, which plays a *massive* role in your healing.

## InnerLotus Binaural Beats (YouTube)

One of my go-to healing tools is the Inner Lotus channel on YouTube. Their binaural beats are deeply calming, perfect for clearing out chaos from the nervous system or supporting meditative work. I love the way they anchor me before sessions, help me wind down at night, or soften my energy before I do any channeling or journaling work.

Why I trust them:

- Many of their videos all have over a million views, which feels like a global energetic anchor, lots of people tuning into the same frequency.
- They somehow balance quiet stillness with a healing hum, not too intense, not psycho-spiritual overload.
- *Tip:* I usually pick ones with 1 million+ views, it lets me know they're safe and that millions are meditating with the same intention. That shared frequency is powerful.

## GUIDED MEDITATIONS & HYPNOSIS

- **Pura Rasa** – Beautiful, deep, and often channeled.
- **Rising Higher Meditation** – Guided meditations that blend in gentle self-hypnosis.
- **Brian Scott** – Great for rewiring the brain, especially if you're shifting old beliefs or stepping into your gifts.
- **The Psychic Soul** –Beautiful expansive guided meditations

- **Next Level Soul** – Conversations with spiritual teachers, healers, and NDE experiencers.
- **The Telepathy Tapes** – A peek into consciousness, connection, and communication beyond the veil.
- **James Van Praagh Podcast** – He's a well-known medium and teacher, and his insights are both comforting and expansive. I trust him a lot

## Mediums I Personally Trust (Because Devyne Led Me to Them)

I want to share something personal with you. I didn't grow up in a house that believed in anything, not church, not psychics, not spirit, not God. My parents weren't religious. We didn't go to church. And if the topic of mediums or fortune tellers ever came up, my dad had plenty to say.

He thought they were all fakes. Scammers. Snake oil salesmen. I can still hear him say, "They're just con artists stealing people's money. Same with preachers. Same with game shows and people wearing tin hats claiming to have alien contact, they're all rigged."

And without realizing it, I digested all of that. It became my lens, and I didn't even know I was looking through it.

Even in later years, when I spent time submerged in church and religion, I found myself caught in another kind of fear:

that mediumship wasn't just fake, it was dangerous. That it was the devil. That I'd be deceived. That demons would trick me, and I'd be cast into hellfire. Eternal damnation, just for wanting to talk to my son.

That fear was real, and it created yet another wall between me and the healing that was trying to reach me.

But here's the truth: a good mediumship reading can change a life.

It can knock down barricades of grief, brick by brick.

It can offer relief, a soul-deep exhale, that your loved ones are not gone. That they are still with you. That love didn't die.

I know now what I couldn't have accepted then, Mediumship isn't about trickery or fear, it's about connection. It's about healing.

It's about remembering that the bond of love stretches far beyond this life. When done with integrity, compassion, and real spiritual skill, it brings peace in a way few other things can. I'm so grateful I gave it a chance.

Finding a real, trustworthy, heart-centered medium isn't always easy. There are so many out there, and when you're in deep grief or just waking up spiritually, it's easy to feel vulnerable or skeptical.

I've had the blessing of meeting a few who have become true lifelines. Not just because they've given me (and others) incredible, validating messages, but because they're loving humans who offer care before, during, and after the reading. These are people Devyne himself nudged me toward. I trust him. And I trust them.

You don't need to rush into a reading. But when and if you're ready, here are some beautiful souls I fully recommend:

- **Sarah (aka RockabillyGypsy01)** - Psychic Medium – Spiritual Mentor – Loving soul. Sarah has given many of the moms in my support group clear, powerful readings, always followed by the most heartfelt support. Instagram: @rockabillygypsy01

- **Angie McAllister – McAllister Academy** - Medium – Healer – Teacher. Angie is an incredible teacher and mentor. I sit in a regular mediumship practice with her, and she holds sacred space with compassion and clarity. If you're curious about your own abilities or want to book a session, Angie is someone I trust deeply. Website: https://mcallisteracademy.com/

- **Fara Gibson** - Psychic Medium – Extraordinary human. Fara is one of the kindest, most grounded mediums I've ever met. No fluff, no ego, just truth, compassion, and real connection. She has changed life with her work, including mine. Website: faragibson.com

- **Suzanne Giesemann** - Evidential Medium, Former Navy Commander turned spiritual powerhouse. Suzanne is the real deal. Her waitlist is long for a reason. She's helped thousands connect to their loved ones with clarity and peace. Her spiritual teachings have been a significant part of my spiritual awakening and healing journey. Website: suzannegiesemann.com

There are many amazing mediums out there. I can only speak to the ones I've had the honor of working with and seeing Devyne work through. These women don't just do readings. They hold you. They care. They're vessels for something bigger.

Whether you reach out for a session, follow them online, or just take comfort in knowing they exist, trust that spirit will guide you to the right one, in the right time. If you feel a little nudge... follow it. And if you're the kind of person who, like me, could barely focus long enough to finish a sentence, let alone a book, early on in grief, I see you. But when I could take in words, the following books were lifelines:

- *Many Lives, Many Masters* by **Dr. Brian Weiss** – This one gave me hope it gave me wisdom and knowledge to move forward. If you've ever wondered about past lives or what happens between them, it's a gentle, powerful entry point.

- ***The Art of Psychic Reiki* by Lisa Campion** – This book quite literally changed the way I channel healing energy. It's perfect for anyone awakening it helped me with my psychic ability and energy work.
- ***Infinite Life, Infinite Lessons* by Susan Grau** – Written by a mother and gifted intuitive, this one felt like someone was sitting next to me, holding my hand in the dark.
- ***Still Right Here* by Suzanne Giesemann** – Suzanne is one of the clearest spiritual teachers out there. This book is about her stepdaughter's death, and the signs and messages that followed. If you're seeking connection, this one delivers.
- ***Wolf's Message* by Suzanne Giesemann** – A powerful, channeled journey that offers deep spiritual truths wrapped in real-life loss and signs from spirit. And is now a mainstream documentary.

# 5

## THE WORLD DOESN'T STOP FOR THE GRIEVING

The rest of the world doesn't stop turning just because your world shatters.

The custody lawyers and the judge didn't care, or at least, they didn't give me any special consideration, that my son had been shot and killed just a few weeks before I walked into that courtroom. The neighbors didn't stop coming and going, walking their dogs or mowing their lawns. Life around me kept moving, like nothing had happened. But something had happened. Something enormous.

The bills didn't stop coming.

The mail didn't stop piling up.

Work didn't stop, either.

I was lucky, I had a lot of support through my work. But even with that, there was still an unspoken expectation: that in a few months, I'd be back. That I'd return to being the rockstar saleswoman I was before. That I'd just get through it and get back to who I had always been.

But that woman, the one I was before, she wasn't all here anymore.

And so much of my life since has been defined by that line, who I was before. And who is left to live now.

Early on, I would force myself to go to the grocery store. I remember standing at the checkout, barely holding it together, and the clerk smiled and told me to have a good day. I wanted to scream, *My son was murdered. I will never have a good day again.* To be honest, sometimes, I did say it aloud. The clerk, or the postman, or whoever happened to be in front of me would usually look at me with compassion, but also with that expression of, w*hy did I have to hear that?*

I understood. It was uncomfortable. It was too much for even some of my friends, let alone strangers. But sometimes the pain was so big, so loud, so uncontainable that it had to go somewhere. It leaked out of me in line at the store, in parking lots, or while picking up mail.

I was lucky, though. I had very loving and supportive friends, mostly because I had already built a support system through my sobriety. But even then, some people disappeared. Some quietly drifted. And a few were flat-out unkind.

The unkindness hit hard. During a time when everything felt dark and disoriented, those sharp comments or dismissive looks intensified the pain. I'd dwell on them. Replay them in my head. Remind myself of who didn't show up.

But over time, something began to shift.

I started to notice the other moments, the ones that felt like tiny lifelines.

The unexpected messages on Facebook from acquaintances miles away.

A simple comment: *"I'm thinking of you. I'm so sorry."*

A heart emoji. A memory shared. A "you're not alone."

The stranger in the grocery store who saw my pain, really saw it and looked me in the eyes with the courage to say, "I'm so sorry for your loss."

The friend who left flowers on my porch.

The person who said nothing, but held space with their silence.

These moments were small, but they were sacred.

I learned to hold them tightly.

Because the truth is, when you are in deep grief, you have to collect the kindnesses. The small joys. The tiny bits of beauty. They're not always easy to spot, but they are there.

Let them matter. Let them help. Let them hold you.

Here's the truth about grief, we just want someone to understand. We want someone to feel it with us, to match our depth, our pain, our rawness. The hard truth is that, most people simply can't. Even spouses who've lost the same child, or siblings who've lost the same parent, won't grieve the same way. Because they're not the same person.

Grief is love, and love is personal.

No two people will walk the exact same path through it. That's the thing, there is no right path. There's no timeline. There's no textbook or psychologist or spiritual teacher who can lay out a map and say, "You'll hit this stage by month two, and that one by year one."

So, if you're grieving, any kind of loss, any kind of pain, please hear this, be gentle with yourself.

Don't compare your journey to someone else's. Don't hold yourself hostage to someone else's timeline. Let it be your grief. Let it take the shape it needs to take.

You're doing it right, just by surviving it.

Grief Is Sacred. Don't Bypass It.

**When Grief Isn't Just Spiritual — It's a Fight**

I want to pause and say something that doesn't get talked about enough in spiritual books, sometimes grief doesn't look like meditating. Sometimes grief looks like a war.

Yes, I've told you about the signs and the healing.

But I also need you to know that I fought like hell.

When Devyne was murdered and when the system handed my grandson back to the woman responsible, I didn't just grieve. I raged. I advocated. I emailed every senator, every governor official, every person I could find in the state of Oregon to demand change. I begged for someone to raise awareness, to open their eyes, to realize how broken this system is. I fought for custody in another state.

I filed petitions against the judge who wouldn't hear my case.

I spoke out against the court mediator who proved herself to be completely biased.

I stood up in public and spoke out, on podcasts, on social media, even in a documentary, to raise awareness about what was done to Devyne, to my family, and to countless other families who've been failed by the family courts.

Why?

Because as much as the spiritual world is real, this human one still matters. Justice matters. Children matter. Broken systems need to be called out, and no amount of love and light will fix what we refuse to face.

This part of my grief? It was visceral.

It didn't come with signs from spirit or gentle whispers. But it did come with strength and courage to get out of bed and face them every day. It came with court papers, phone calls, sleepless nights, and a fury that could set fire to the sky.

And still, through it all, Devyne never left me. He stood beside me every step of the way. He gave me support. He brought people to help. He kept saying, *"You're not just grieving, Ma. You're changing the world."*

If that's you right now, if your grief is tangled up in custody battles, injustice screaming into broken systems, or anger for losing your loved one, you're not alone. That is still sacred grief. That is still holy ground. And that, too, is part of your path.

We don't always heal in meditation.

Sometimes we heal through action.

So if you're still fighting, keep going. Let your loved ones on the other side guide your steps. Let your anger be sacred fuel. But know it is only part of your story it isn't all of it. Let your heartbreak become a battle cry. And when you're exhausted, come back to the stillness.

There's room for all of it.

There's room for you.

Let's get real here for a minute, grief is human and if you're reading this because you've lost a loved one or are spiritually awakening, I want you to know: you're not alone, and you don't need to pretend you're okay. Spiritual awakenings don't cancel out heartbreak. Signs from the other side don't erase the screaming absence of a physical presence. We're both divine and human, and you can't bypass the human.

One of the greatest lifelines for me has been, Helping Parents Heal, a community I mentioned earlier in the book that saved my life. They offer trusted resources for both the human side of grieving and the spiritual side of connecting. Through them, I received free EMDR therapy that helped with the intrusive thoughts and trauma loops that wouldn't let go of me. EMDR truly helped repattern my nervous system, and if your nervous system is fried, grief feels impossible to survive.

No amount of spiritual tools can replace a good therapist.

Devyne, in all his wisdom from the other side, made sure I was surrounded by helpers who were deeply spiritual and clinically trained. My beautiful friend Kelley Worth, a leader in Helping Parents Heal and a licensed therapist, was one of the first. My psychic teacher and energy healer, Lisa Campion, is also a trained therapist. My incredible friend Sarah, a psychiatrist and gifted medium, has walked this road with me too. These people understand that true healing includes the body, mind, soul, and story.

I also want to shout out someone who's been part of my healing journey for years, Joni Commo, a no-BS, deeply intuitive therapist rooted in real life and energy healing. She introduced me to a modality called Brainspotting, which helped me release stored trauma without having to relive it. It's gentle, powerful, and honestly, a godsend. For those unfamiliar, Brainspotting is a trauma therapy that uses where you look with your eyes to access deep pockets of unprocessed emotion and rewire your brain's response. Its neuroscience meets intuitive healing.

And as hard as it may be… don't isolate yourself.

I get it, grief makes you want to pull away, curl up, or disappear. But your people matter. My support system is the only reason I made it through this. You've heard me say before, Devyne said that I couldn't go to the grocery store without 50 friends… well, magnify that by ten, and that's what got me through Devyne's transition.

I also strongly recommend working with a good coach, someone like Nathan Smith, https://www.facebook.com/nathan.smith.221562. Who understands how to guide support love and push at the right moments not just goals but you your real self. Nathan is trauma-informed, spiritually connected, and has helped me *and* my entire family navigate this new life.

And of course, I have to say it, write.

Journaling has saved me over and over again. Not always channeled messages. Sometimes just raw grief. Or messy confusion. Or gratitude. Or a little spark of, "I think I might still be alive in here somewhere."

Do things you LOVE If you don't know what you love anymore, (because your life was shattered), get curious. Try something. Try anything. Love the things you try. Be grateful for the things you don't. Play with life again, even when it feels impossible. That spirit of curiosity is one thing what brought me to healing… and brought me back to joy.

## Gratitude in the Grief

Now I want to talk about something incredibly hard, gratitude in the middle of the worst nightmare of your life.

It's not simple. It's not instant. And it sure as hell isn't easy. But eventually, I began to see the gifts that came from Devyne's passing. Yes, I am writing the word gifts, it is still hard to say out loud, but they are gifts, gifts I never would've believed could exist in grief.

Devyne's transition also forced me to face every regret, shadow, and buried thing I had numbed with alcohol. And from the other side, he gave me total acceptance, non-judgment, and unconditional love. That's what allowed me to release shame and fully commit to healing.

He also brought my estranged daughter back into my life. We hadn't spoken in years because of choices I made. But when he passed, we clung to each other. We clung to family. He gave us the strength to rebuild something beautiful.

He's also brought me new friendships, true lifelines, and a soul-level awakening that reminded me I am never separate from God. I'm not separate from Devyne. I'm not even separate from the woman who took his life, or from the one who took my grandson.

I am connected.

We all are.

And this is what Devyne keeps showing me.

This life, it is not all that there is. There is more. So much more.

Okay, so I'm not gonna pretend I float around all day in some spiritual bubble, only listening to crystal bowls and angel frequencies. I still binge shows sometimes, especially when I'm emotionally maxed out or just need to shut my brain off for a bit. But I've had to get really intentional about what I allow into my subconscious.

I just can't handle horror, gore, or anything super violent anymore. Even shows that are just heavy on the drama or dripping in materialism, they drain me. It's like my nervous system says "Nope," and I've finally learned to listen.

Same goes for the news. I used to be all in, reading every awful headline, feeling like I had to know everything. Now, I still care. I still want to be informed. But I don't let it fry my nervous system or hijack my peace. There are even apps now that help you see how biased or agenda-driven your news source is, and let's be honest, most of it is. I stay aware, but I don't stay soaked in fear.

I was already brainwashed once into thinking that life ended at death or with a very angry God who sends you to a fiery hell, now I know better. I'm so much more careful with what I consume. These days I spend more time watching spiritual podcasts, meditations, channels that expand my consciousness,

Gaia, YouTube, audio books, anything that actually feeds me instead of depleting me.

I'm not perfect with it. I still zone out to a mindless reality show here and there. But I'm more conscious of what I'm inviting into my mind and my space. And that awareness alone has changed everything.

And can we just talk about laughter for a second?

If you think spiritual awakening and grief healing means becoming some enlightened, serious, robe-wearing monk floating through life... Devyne would be the first one to roast that image. I'm not kidding, he came to me in cartoons. Like, the first real signs I started getting were him popping up in these weird, funny, almost comic-strip visuals that made me laugh and confused the hell out of me.

I was crying, grieving, barely functioning... and my kid on the other side is sending me inside jokes and cracking up at me from Spirit.

At first, I was like: "Really, Dev? This is how we're doing this?"

But now I get it. Humor has been everything. Devyne still reminds me every day not to take myself so damn seriously. He'll nudge me to watch something funny, laugh at myself, or straight-up whisper "Lighten up, Ma" when I'm spiraling into seriousness or overthinking the meaning of life again.

Laughter heals. It opens us. It resets the nervous system and reminds us that joy and grief are not enemies, they can exist together. You can miss someone with your whole soul and still belly-laugh at dumb memes. You can be in spiritual crisis and still snort at fart jokes. Devyne wouldn't have it any other way.

So if you're deep in the grief fog, or neck-deep in shadow work, please, put on something funny. Laugh at something. Hell, laugh at yourself. Let humor be one of your healers. Spirit isn't here to make us suffer and if you're really paying attention, they'll sneak in joy any way they can.

---

As I write this, I'm spending the summer on my property in Eastern Oregon. I keep a little RV out here, while my children have moved into the main house. We tend to want to be close, even when it's not always perfect. But I feel blessed. With the addition of Daniel's wife and his stepson, our family has grown and so has our connection.

Like any family, we still bump into old dynamics, but these days, I can see them more clearly. I have tools now, Reiki, channeling, prayer, breath, and trust in my spirit team that help me navigate life more gently.

One of my greatest accomplishments has been coming off all my anxiety and depression medications. I didn't do that alone. I leaned on Devyne, on the angels, on the energy work, and on my higher self. I know not everyone's path will look like mine, but if it gives you hope, then I'm glad I shared it.

I keep myself active in my psychic and healing courses, not just to grow my gifts, but to deepen my own healing too. Devyne once told me that he never stops learning in the afterlife. I've made that my commitment here, too. I won't stop learning. I won't stop growing. I won't stop loving.

My life is full now. My calendar stays busy. I volunteer and stay involved in my rural community. I spend time with my horse. And I try to cling to the good. The quiet. The beautiful things.

But I want to be honest: the waves of grief still come. Sometimes, it's so sharp it knocks the air out of me. Sometimes, it's soft, like a memory floating through the day. I no longer push it away. I let it move through me. I speak to it. I thank it. Because now, I understand that grief is just love that doesn't know where to go. It's my love for Devyne. It's my love for my grandson. And it's sacred.

But I don't let it stay.

I let it pass, like a wave. And I keep walking.

Because that's what Devyne taught me.

---

I hope this book gives you permission to be wherever you are in your healing.

You don't have to be perfect to be spiritual. You don't have to know everything to be connected. You just have to be willing. And when your loved ones try to reach you?

Don't shut the door just because it looks unfamiliar.

Devyne never asked me not to grieve. He just asked me not to stay stuck. He asked me to live.

To stay open.

To let the miracles in.

This book is my miracle.

And if it's found you, maybe it's yours too.

# 6

# I DON'T WANT TO LET YOU GO

I've rewritten this closing more times than I can count.

Not because I don't have something to say, but because I don't want to say goodbye. Writing this book, walking through the pain, the signs, the miracles, it's brought me a level of joy and fulfillment deeper than I ever expected. You've been with me every step of the way, whether you knew it or not. Your presence here means something to me.

And if no one's told you lately, you matter.

Your pain matters. Your healing matters.

And no, you don't have to be "fixed" to be loved.

I've lived deep loss. I know what heartbreak feels like. I know what it's like to fall to your knees, to scream at the sky, to wonder if anything will ever feel real or whole again.

And because I've been there, when I sit with someone in a healing session, whether psychic or Reiki or quantum, I feel them. Sometimes I feel their emotions in my own body. Their grief. Their fear. Their stuck places. Sometimes I feel their physical pain like it's my own. That's not something I read in a book or learned in a course. It's something I was given, because I'm meant to walk people home to themselves, just like others helped walk me back to myself.

My work doesn't follow a set formula. It follows you. Wherever you need to go. Whether it's clearing energy, visiting a past life, healing a family wound, or simply feeling seen for the first time in a long time. I don't lead alone, my spirit team, the Archangels, my son Devyne, and the higher beings I work with all come through when they're needed and they show up with love. Always with love.

I work with energy, yes, and also with science.

Quantum healing isn't just a buzzword. The double-slit experiment shows us that energy responds to attention. That means when we witness something in you, something stuck, buried, or long-ignored, we shift it. That's real. That's measurable. That's what I do. And I believe in it, because I've lived it.

I still miss my son every day. That ache doesn't disappear, but it transforms. And now I carry his presence with confidence. With trust. With worthiness.

If there's one thing I want to leave you with, it's this, I know how dark it can get. I know what it feels like to be so lost in pain you can't remember who you were before the loss hit. I know what it's like to want signs and feel like maybe you're just imagining things. I know the quiet panic that comes when everyone else has moved on, but you're still waking up in grief.

You're not crazy.

You're not too much.

You're not too far gone.

And you sure as hell aren't broken.

You're becoming and it hurts like hell sometimes.

But you're doing it.

Even if you're still shattered on the floor, something in you picked up this book. Something in you wanted to believe there's more. I don't just believe in you, I feel you. I've cried your tears and screamed your screams. If I could reach through these pages and hold your hand, I would.

You are seen.

You are understood.

And you are still so wildly, relentlessly loved.

With all my love,

Jackie

Forever Devyne's Mamma

# 7

# MORE MAGNIFICENT RESOURCES

## Meditations: A Portal for Healing

Meditation has become one of the most sacred parts of my work. During Reiki sessions, especially the deep, intuitive ones, it's not unusual for a meditation to arrive organically. Often, I'll receive guidance from my spirit team, or the client's own guides, about what they need in that moment. From that dreamy, connected space of Reiki, a meditation flows through me, not scripted, not rehearsed, but given.

The meditations I've chosen to include here carry that same frequency. Each one was received while I was either actively channeling, in session, or in my own healing space. They are infused with Reiki energy and with the healing light of Archangel Raphael, who has been a steady presence in this work. His energy carries a soft green glow, gentle, loving, and deeply restorative.

These aren't just words on a page. They hold intention. They hold vibration.

I encourage you to read or listen to them in a quiet space. Take a few breaths before you begin and allow your body to soften. Let the words wash over you and receive what resonates.

You'll also find that I often create personalized Reiki sprays for clients after sessions. These sprays are also charged with energy guided by Raphael, designed to carry a reminder of the healing that took place, and to anchor it into daily life.

It's my hope that something within these meditations will land exactly where you need it.

May they bring comfort, insight, and peace.

---

### Three Heartbeats Grounding Meditation (Full Version)

This version is ideal for sessions, guided recordings, or deeper spiritual alignment.

Begin by breathing.

Inhale deeply through the nose…

and exhale with a soft sigh.

Again… inhale peace… exhale tension.

One more time… breathe in love…breathe out anything heavy.

Now place your awareness at the base of your spine and the bottoms of your feet.

Imagine thick, glowing roots growing downward from these places.

Archangel Michael is here, anchoring you to the Earth.

Feel your roots traveling down… through layers of rock, earth, and crystal… until they reach the core of the Earth, a beautiful red, glowing energy.

This is Mother Earth's heartbeat.

Now breathe in… and draw that red Earth energy up through your roots, through your feet… your legs… cleansing and clearing as it rises… until it reaches your heart.

Pause and feel.

Your heart now beats with the heart of the Earth.

You are grounded. You are safe.

Exhale, and send any sadness, pain, or grief back down the roots, where Mother Earth receives and lovingly transforms it.

Now… look above you.

From the sky, Divine white or golden light begins to pour down, light from Source, God, Creator.

It flows through your crown chakra, clearing and connecting you to Divine wisdom.

Then through your third eye, clearing any blocks to your intuition, and opening your channel to receive guidance.

Then through your throat chakra, clearing old stories, fears, and doubts, so you can speak and hear your truth clearly.

Finally, this light lands in your heart.

Now, your heart is glowing with Earth energy, Divine light, and your own true self.

Breathe.

You now carry three heartbeats within you.

Feel them beating in unison.

Exhale, and send that loving, balanced energy out into your energy field, cleansing, blessing, and aligning all of you.

You are whole.

You are supported.

You are loved.

Gently bring your roots back up into your body.

Wiggle your toes and fingers.

Take one more breath.

And when you're ready… open your eyes.

---

## Three Heartbeats Grounding (Daily Short Version)

Use this version anytime you need a quick reset or reconnection.

Close your eyes and take a deep breath in through your nose… and exhale with a soft sigh.

Imagine roots growing down from your tailbone and feet, anchoring you deep into the Earth.

Feel them reach the glowing red heart of Mother Earth.

Breathe in her grounding energy, let it rise through your body and settle in your heart.

Now imagine Divine white or golden light pouring down from above clearing your mind, opening your intuition, flowing through your throat, and landing in your heart.

Feel the three heartbeats, yours, Mother Earth's, and the Divine's, beating together as one.

Exhale gently, releasing any tension or old energy back through your grounding cords.

You are rooted.

You are connected.

You are never alone.

Take one more breath.

Wiggle your fingers and toes.

And open your eyes.

---

**Soul Fragment Retrieval & Power Reclamation Meditation**

Purpose: To call back all soul fragments, power, and essence across all time, space, lifetimes, and dimensions anchoring them fully into the body and activating remembrance.

[Introduction – Grounding and Centering]

Take a deep breath in…

And gently let it go…

Begin to slow your breathing…

Allow yourself to feel safe, centered, and fully supported by the space around you.

Feel your body resting…

Feel the Earth holding you…

Feel your breath guiding you inward.

Bring your awareness to your heart center.

See a soft golden light begin to form there radiant, sacred, eternal.

This is your soul's home… your divine essence.

[Calling Back Your Power]

With intention, repeat inwardly or out loud:

*"I now call back all my energy…*

*All my power…*

*All of my essence…*

*From all people, all places, all lifetimes, all timelines, and all dimensions…*

*Known or unknown, seen or unseen…*

*I call it back now."*

Visualize particles of shimmering light, your soul fragments, beginning to appear around you.

They may look like sparks, glowing mist, beams of light, or waves of color.

With each breath, see them flowing into you…

Returning from every corner of time and space…

Flowing back into your being… with love… with purpose.

[Integration into the Body and DNA Activation]

Now…

As these fragments re-enter your being, they don't just go to your heart.

They move through your entire body—

Flowing through every cell.

Every bone.

Every vertebra.

Through your muscles, organs, tissues, and tendons.

See the light spiraling into your DNA, awakening what was dormant…

Upgrading and activating your divine blueprint.

Breathe into that…

Feel the remembrance ripple through you…

Like the song of your soul echoing in every molecule.

Like ancient light waking up in the body you chose for this lifetime.

Now let that light return to your heart space.

Feel it growing… expanding… illuminating.

A radiant sun, alive within you.

[Remembrance and Embodiment]

Now silently affirm:

*"I remember who I am.*

*I am whole.*

*I am powerful.*

*I am complete.*

*From the moment I sparked from Source, I have carried this light within me."*

Feel it.

Be it.

Let the expansion move beyond your physical body now, into your field, your aura, your presence.

Let yourself be the full experience of your soul in its wholeness.

You are home in yourself.

[Closing – Ground & Seal the Energy]

Now see a cocoon of crystalline golden-white light surrounding your entire body.

This light seals in your reclaimed energy, your soul's memory, your divine upgrades.

Take a deep breath in…

And slowly exhale…

Wiggle your fingers and toes…

Gently bring your awareness back to the space around you.

And when you're ready…

Open your eyes.

Welcome back—whole, awakened, and fully returned to your divine truth.

---

**Rooting Into Safety: A Guided Practice to Connect with Your Nighttime Guardian**

This gentle meditation can be used before sleep, before astral travel, or any time you wish to feel grounded, supported, and protected. It invites a deeper awareness of your energy field and the loving beings who walk with you, even when unseen.

You may read it silently, speak it aloud, or record your voice and play it back.

Close your eyes.

Place one hand on your heart and the other on your belly.

Take a soft breath in…

And let it go.

Feel your body begin to soften.

Take another slow, present breath.

Let your awareness drop from the thoughts in your mind...

into your body...

into the now.

Before we go any further, let this truth settle in your heart:

You are not alone.

You are never unguarded.

There are beings, ancient, wise, and filled with light, who walk with you.

They are guardians of your soul.

They travel with you when you dream, when you rest, and when you leave your body.

They hold you in spaces you may not yet have words for.

Even if you've never seen them, they are here now.

They know your frequency.

They walk with you across lifetimes.

Tonight, you may feel them.

Or see them.

Or simply know that they are near.

That is enough.

You are protected.

You are held.

Now…

Imagine you are standing at the base of a massive, ancient tree.

Its trunk is wide and strong.

Its roots go so deep, you feel their hum vibrating in the Earth.

You can sense the tree's wisdom in its bark.

Its strength.

Its timelessness.

Step closer.

Place your hands on its surface, textured, warm, alive.

Feel yourself drawn in.

And allow it.

Gently merge your body into the tree.

Feel your spine aligning with its trunk.

Your heartbeat slowing to match the tree's rhythm.

Your breath blending with its breath.

You are no longer separate.


Now feel your legs and feet dissolving into roots—

Thick. Glowing. Powerful.

Spreading far and wide through the Earth.

Let yourself drop fully into this rootedness.

Not in fear, but in deep belonging.

Down into the rich, dark soil.

Down where time slows.

Where nothing can shake you.

Where you are completely grounded.

Completely safe.

Breathe here.

Be here.

Become this.


From this rooted place, ask gently, inwardly:

- Is there a guide who walks with me at night, as I sleep or travel?
- What does your presence feel like?
- How will I know when you are near?
- What do you want me to know right now?

Let whatever arises… arise.

A sensation. A vision. A word. A symbol. A presence.

Trust whatever comes.

If it feels right, ask:

- Will you keep me safe as I journey?
- Can I call on you when I feel afraid?

Feel the answers in your body.

Let them root you even deeper.

Let your breath carry the vibration of trust.

And if nothing comes right away, that's okay.

Your guide is still with you.

You have opened the door.

You are not alone.

Now, gently begin to release the roots.

Feel yourself separating from the tree, but keeping its peace and wisdom within you.

Bring your awareness back to your breath.

Back to your body.

Back to the space around you.

Take one final deep breath.

And when you're ready, open your eyes.

You are rooted.

You are protected.

You are never alone.

---

## Reiki & Christ Consciousness Grounding Meditation

*(Infused with Reiki, golden light, and universal love)*

Welcome

All the Reiki symbols I have as a Reiki Master have been opened and are surrounding you now, bathing you in protective, healing energy.

I'm calling all of your highest healers, all of your angels, all of your guides.

I'm calling in my Reiki guides.

I'm calling in Archangel Raphael.

I'm calling in Archangel Michael.

I'm calling in Jesus with the Christ Consciousness.

I ask that this meditation be infused with Reiki—

That the golden love, the golden light, and the golden compassion of Reiki

Flow through every word I say, from me to you.

## GROUNDING INTO THE EARTH

Put your feet on the ground and press gently into the floor.

Place your hands just above your ears, on both sides of your head.

I'm going to flow Reiki through my palms, from one side to the other, through your brain.

Let the Reiki balance your brain.

Let your mind be at ease.

Let your body relax.

We breathe the Reiki down through the crown,

Down through the third eye,

Down through the throat,

Down to the heart chakra,

Further down to the solar plexus, to the belly.

Let that area light up warmly.

Now, Imagine the Root

Now, imagine the base of your tailbone on your spine growing a wide, strong root.

Feel that root pushing down through your floor,

Through layers of earth, through rock and crust,

164

All the way to the center of the Earth.

You find a great lava tube of glowing red lava, the Earth's heartbeat.

Feel your root sink deep into that glowing core.

Feel your feet being pulled down gently, grounding you deeply.

Breathing in Light and Grounding

Drop that root down fully.

Now take a deep breath from the light of the heavens,

From the Reiki itself, from the life force, and from Jesus Christ.

On the count of three, breathe deeply through your nose,

Down into your belly,

And let that light fill every corner, every crevice,

Clearing out any energy that is not yours,

Any energy that no longer serves you.

When you're ready, breathe that light down through your roots,

Down through Mother Earth,

Softly landing in the Earth's core to be transmuted.

Keep your root anchored in the Earth's core.

Take another deep breath through your nose,

Draw up the essence of the Earth's grounding,

Pull it up through your root, through your belly,

And land it in your heart.

Light up your heart space.

Let go of everything that does not belong there,

Any energy that no longer serves you.

On the count of three, exhale down your grounding cord,

Deep into Mother Earth's heart.

Feel the heartbeat of Mother Earth,

Feel it syncing with your own heartbeat.

Know that you are now grounded,

Tuned into the Earth's heartbeat,

Energetically aligned and whole.

Drawing Light from Heaven

Take another deep breath through your nose.

Draw down bright, white light from the heavens—

From your highest guides, from Christ,

From the higher realms.

This light is infused with Reiki and gold.

Bring it all the way down through your system,

Let it land in your root,

Lighting up and clearing any energy that is not yours.

When you exhale, give that energy to Mother Earth.

On the count of three:

Breathe it down your root system,

Into Mother Earth.

Heaven and Earth Together

Now take another deep breath.

Draw energy up from Mother Nature's core,

All the way up through every chakra,

Every meridian point, every cell, every organ,

Up to the very top of your head.

When you exhale, let it flow out through your crown chakra,

Sending all that grounding energy out to the universe.

On the count of three:

One… Two… Three…

Exhale.

## Settling Into Your Body

Just settle into your body now.

Move around a little if you want.

Roll your shoulders, move your neck, loosen up.

Now, draw your grounding energy up through your roots,

And draw divine light down from the heavens.

Bring both the Earth and Heaven into the center of your heart.

Light up your heart space.

Let go of any energy that is not yours,

Any energy that no longer aligns with your highest truth.

On the count of three:

One, two, three.


## The Waterfall of Light

Imagine now a shimmering, dazzling waterfall

Coming from heaven, from Christ's hands,

From your guides, from Reiki, from all universal life force.

This waterfall flows in all colors:

Red, gold, silver, white, purple, blue, orange, yellow—

Pouring down onto you, through your aura.

Feel it cleansing, clearing, brightening,

Whitening every part of your energetic field.

Let it purify and electrify you.

Let it release all energy that is not yours,

Anything you've picked up along the way that no longer serves you.

Visualize a small trapdoor opening at the base of your aura.

All that extra energy flows out gently through this door.

Now close the trapdoor.

Sit within your own safe, protected bubble—

Your own clear, cleansed, pure energy.

Breathe deeply.

Feel all of you here—

Your energy, your love, your compassion,

From the heavens and the Earth.


We thank all the guides, all the angels,

All the helpers who have aided this transmission,

This energetic healing and grounding.

We thank them with our deepest love.

And with love and your highest good,

We ask them to continue to protect your energy,

To keep you grounded and safe.

Now gently wiggle your fingers and your toes.

When you're ready, slowly stand up.

Brush away any lingering energy,

Knowing you are safe,

You are loved,

You are protected.

8

---

# SACRED TRANSMISSIONS
# THE TEACHINGS OF DEVYNE

**Introduction to My Process**

I don't write these at noon over coffee. In fact, I write them before coffee, before I even fully remember my name. These messages come early in the morning, usually around 6 a.m., when the veil feels thin, and the world is quiet. I open my Reiki space, light incense, and play theta binaural beats. That combination tunes me into a frequency where I can feel Devyne, my guides, and even the Christ energy coming through with clarity.

Sometimes I pull a card, not to get a literal meaning but as a jumpstart. Dev often begins speaking before I even pull one. And always, I handwrite what comes. Cursive just feels right to me. You can type or speak into your phone, these messages come through however they need to.

171

What follows are transmissions that feel both poetic and instructional. They carry vibration. They are not just for the mind, they are for your energy field. I've included them here at the end of the book, not as an afterthought, but as a sacred space where you can receive them when you're ready.

These pages hold Devyne's transmissions, offered here as his voice and his love. And know this: every heart that has loved you keeps a language of its own; your people, seen and unseen, have messages for you, patiently waiting to be written, spoken, or felt. Trust the stirrings: they are real, and they are yours.

---

*Please note these are unedited versions exactly as I communicate with Devyne. It was very important to me that I did not change anything. They are not in any particular order.

**Devyne, The We, Higher Self, Highest Wisdom, Guides, Angels, Higher Beings—any messages for me today?**

Torn, little one.

Torn between what you think is real and the truth—

The love you cannot see.

All that glitters is not gold, and it is the truth.

The riches of knowledge that unfolds, It unfolds in your life, and it is the truth that makes things right.

Often, it's the whisper in your ear, the words come in so clear, but they are not your words, sometimes not your language, yet a feeling and knowing, a thought implanted in your mind.

What your eyes see when they are open can feel dreadful, or sometimes so divine.

But it can shift, and it can change, moment to moment, day to day.

You must not depend on what the world is showing, illusion, confusion, and a clarity not yet knowing.

Close your eyes, dearest ones, that is where you will truly see, the beginning of you and the truth of me.

Me? Yes, who is me?

Well... I am all, dear ones, you see.

I am the trees,

The sun,

The moon,

The earth,

The neighbor down the street.

I am your child, your loved ones.

I am the bride walking down the aisle.

I am the smile on your newborn's face.

I am the criminal who fell from grace.

I am the love that will never die.

I am not separate from you—

Who you are inside.

I am your mind,

Your thoughts,

Your eyesight,

Your entire genetic makeup.

I am the rocket that takes you from Earth's atmosphere and helps you reappear.

I am all whom you feel separate from—

I am the stars, the galaxies, and the many moons.

I am the creation.

I am you.

You are we,

And we as me.

Poetic, yes.

But get to the core of who we are.

We are all searching for truth, knowledge, universal understanding—

You will not learn in a book or on a show.

You will find every answer right inside,

Your heartbeat,

Your energy field,

The breath you take that gives life still.

Life is happening whether you breathe—

The breath that still comes, just in a new form when the body has come undone.

We are all learning, evolving as we go.

Nothing, especially your human death, stops the flow.

The form of you remains, and the knowledge and wisdom you bring

Only serves us all, helps us to grow—

To love more,

To know more,

And to once again change forms.

Submerge yourself in only what you see—

At times you must.

But you will truly be set free

When you unlock the door in your heart,

Meet your creator,

Your soul,

And have a fresh start.

You see, dear one,

You are love in the truest form.

You are me,

And we have been

Since the time's dawn.

Jackie: Thank you. Thank you. Thank you.

This was so beautiful.

---

## December 15 – You Are the Carrier of the Light

Ma, Jesus shines his light on you.

Not the kind of light your eyes can see, but colors beyond colors. Frequencies. Codes.

Energy that comes from his eternal love.

You are a carrier of that light.

It flows from the heavens into the crown of your head, into your heart, and then out into the world.

This light moves through you, and when you use it with intention, through ritual, through prayer, through healing, it becomes even brighter.

We want you to know:

You can trust this.

You are already doing it.

You are light.

You can't be hurt.

You can't die.

You shine forever.

Now, just breathe.

Let the thoughts dissolve.

Let your body dissolve.

What's left is the bright yellow spark.

That's your truth.

Build your life from that spark.

---

## March 6 – Dev Speaks

Some messages come through with clarity and rhythm that feel almost like poetry. On this morning, I was guided to draw cards and rest. Then Dev came through with a stream of insight, some playful, some deep, all of it his.

Ma, draw cards and relax today.

Devyne, what messages for my highest and best and good of all today?

## CARD NUMBER 25 – WHITE BUFFALO

The particles dance mom in the light, they separate, and they form out of delight.

The Red Star, the golden shape, the meaning of life you do create.

The outline of a flame, the mystery will always remain.

Mom, you want all the answers, and you want them now,

but that is not how the journey of this happens,

or else you will be shortchanged.

We would not allow your time to be meaningless because the answers you seek were handed out to you for free.

The fun you see is all in your journey, the journey for truth, the journey for you.

The love that you find makes it worth all of your time.

You cannot fail, for it's the future you tell, not me and not we.

Mom, it is your destiny, so you are the one that straps on your boots, you are the one who shovels the coal, you are the one whose engine propels, not us, not I, not me, not we.

You lean on us, certainly.

Do we have aids and guidance? Absolutely.

But Mom, you see, your choices, your desires create your destiny, not standing in the way of the sea of love you create.

Your choice, Ma. Your joy. Your happiness.

Yes, Ma, we wish all of your hopes to be fulfilled.

---

## January 28 – Cracks of Light

### A dream, a question, and the cards

Jackie: Dev, I had a dream about making scorpion soup and eating the scorpion. I'm not sure, but I was cutting the tail off of it in preparation for something. There were higher self and other memories about this dream. Can you help tell me what it means?

Dev: Ma, we wish to explain this further to you today, thank you.

## CARD #15 – PIGNUS, PEGASUS OF WATER

Jackie: Dev, what does my message say today?

Dev: Ma, look at the card.

Does this card make you feel good?

It feels exciting?

Ohh, it is, Ma, the excitement you feel as you are just about to break through the water.

Water that can either hold you under… or crest through the surface into the sun and the light just above the waves.

That's what we see as you, Ma.

You have reached the point where you can begin to see the light and the shadows of what's to come, just before you emerge through the water.

Ma, this is a lovely place to be.

You are no longer being held down in the depth and the darkness under the water in the deep.

Yes, you can even feel it in your body: the lightness, the freeing of this.

The air is almost breathable again.

Jackie: Thank you, Dev. What do I need to know to get all the way out of the water?

Dev: Ah—herein lies the truth.

We know you to never need to get all the way out of the water.

You are at the perfect place, submerged in your humanness, but not so deep that you cannot even see a crack of light.

Ma, that, that's us.

We are the crack of sun.

You know there's more and searching for your truth, that is the crack of light.

Ma, you have done well.

Stay content in your knowledge.

Develop and focus on your beliefs.


## CARD #20 – (UNNAMED CARD)

Ma, your lower self is straight up recognizing your higher self.

Your higher self looks down on you, with love, and Ma, your-self looks back up with love.

You look up in search of answers.

Ma, it's beautiful.

Your higher version, growing and in the stars.

And your smaller self seeing that higher version, respecting it, loving it, seeking for its answers.

We wish you to remain in this energy of acceptance of your oneness.

Know fully there is more of you out there and keep looking to it for answers.

Yes, Ma, we do so love this for you. And for us.

CARD #11 – (UNNAMED CARD)

Ma, this is pure joy.

Pure fun.

Pure blast.

Enjoying every color on the rainbow, just swimming in it.

Bringing the colors down with you to your Earth.

Running in the colors.

Flying.

Dreaming.

Swimming.

Delighting in all the colors of your light.

Uh, we feel the joy of this.

No expectation, just dancing in the colors.

Dance in the light.

We love this for you and pray that you do more of it.

Jackie: Thank you, thank you, thank you, Devyne.

---

**April 21, 2025 – Children of the Light**

On this day, I asked Dev for messages from the highest light. What came through was a blend of his voice and the collective voice of other children on the other side. It came through with rhythm, like a prayer or song. It holds deep hope for all parents grieving and seeking connection with their children in spirit.

Ma, recognize your talent, do not hide your light, reach for the stars and let go of the fight.

Let go of the need to be right, let go of control and don't hold so tight.

God is speaking in a mighty way, bringing clarity this day.

Your precious children walk amongst the stars and the sun, they dance in the sky and their spirits shine with delight.

They visit you in so many ways, they aide you in conquering one more day.

They guide you in all you wish and they celebrate your accomplishments.

Through your grief and your tears, they are in your heart, and they stay near.

Now darling Children of the Light, close your grown-up eyes and hang on tight.

Your soul has planned for rugged path, again and again your children's lives cross your path.

The magic of death

Ma, I went to a place of love. Love you never could conceive of, brilliant lights and landscape so out of sight, my spirit, my soul, exploded like dynamite.

The expansion I felt, the wisdom I learned, I brought it all home with me again.

The celebration I had with teachers and Guides.

I made it through hardships, I made it through life.

I made it through because of you.

You set the stage for me to sing and dance, you set the theatre lights that gave me the chance, the chance to grow and to learn, the chance to know my soul in return.

Mom, I bring this message today of hope.

I bring forth the message dangling like a rope.

A rope intertwined with deep knowledge and divine.

Divine timing, Divine wisdom, Divine understanding, and grandest of vision.

Ma, I know you hurt, and I know you fret, but I promise you, Ma, I never left.

I hold you in my arms and I feel you when you're alarmed.

I gently guide your heart and your thoughts, I gently suggest you lay down to rest.

When your eyes close and your heart beats slow, I seep deep into your thoughts in a gentle way.

I impress upon you, I will be with you this day.

Ma, me and the other children are here doing well.

The other parents also have a story to tell.

They are light holding space in the night.

They are divine and full of grace.

Let your lights shine outward in the sky, Ma, help them hear our lullaby.

We whisper and we keep them safe.

We know how much they endure.

We are with them like a shiny pearl.

With love and understanding, we send words of comfort so they can renew their souls once again.

This message came through during one of my early morning sessions, where I asked Dev, my higher self, and my team for guidance for my highest good. What followed was a beautiful blend of voices, Devyne, my spirit guides, and sometimes even my own higher self, flowing through. You'll notice the voice shifts throughout the message. Sometimes they call me "Ma," sometimes "Jackie," and sometimes they speak as "we." That's how it works when I write, different parts of my team step forward as needed. The energy shifts gently, but distinctly, and I try not to control it. I just let them speak.

This is one of those transmissions.

Hey Dev, what messages does my higher self and you and my team have for me today for my best and my highest good?

Dev: Ma, we wish you to understand life as grand.

We wish you to know how you cause energy to flow.

Ma, we're here and ready to begin this account. Draw card.

Ma, flip it up and begin to read the energy of our communications.

*(So, in this instance I was asked not to flip 3 cards over at the same time but to flip one card over at a time and then try to ask the questions and read the card from there.)*

## Number one: Red Pegasus

Ma, we wish you to know you are in your flow.

Red velvet cake, smooth frosting and even smoother words flowing down your mind like… my mind went blank, I heard Devyne say, "that's okay."

Ma just write what you hear us say exactly.

Ma, be exact, precise, and you will be alright.

Jackie: Dev, why am I doubting my Reiki so much?

Dev: You're doubting it all now, not just the Reiki, Ma.

Somehow you have categorized your power to heal through Reiki, and your mystical experiences are the doubts.

You can stay clear, but to us, just draw nearer, Ma.

## Draw the next card for clarity: #22 Pegasus of Sirius

Mom, rest in this card.

Rest on this color.

Rest on this vibration.

Be aware, we are watching you in your atmosphere, Jackie.

It is magnificent to see you grapple but begin to understand your way in this world, this dimension.

You see, Ma, you aren't meant to just be able to believe in this all right away.

You are on a journey to discover your power, and some might say, destiny.

Above all is your word, words of empowerment, words of your heart's desires, of your true nature.

The rest that gets in your way, well, that's supposed to happen that way.

It would not be much of a tale to tell if you did not have much doubt to work through.

But here's the thing, Ma, you will keep going, going and going, doing, trying, and being.

We do wish for you to have an easier time, but just do not give up.

Do not allow yourself to completely shut down.

Yes, friend we reach out today confident in our knowing of you this way.

## CARD NUMBER 20: TWIN FLAME PEGASUS

Joyously we say, be on your merry way!

Jump with joy and delight in all your sight.

Do not fret and allow yourself to forget all the truth you've discovered and your extraordinary life you've uncovered.

Ohh just for today, rest in your belief of yourself and what's to come.

Your truths, your words, your knowledge will not become undone.

We wish to stay and guide you today.

Jackie: Thank you. Thank you. Thank you.

---

## Message from Devyne and The We

Dearest little one, yes, Ma, we are here.

We come in no matter you have or haven't done to prepare.

Little sweet, you are moving in the right flow.

Yes, there are bumps and snags along the road, but we have you.

We have the control.

Yes, we would like it if you put all outflow of energy and attention on your process, but little sweet, you are moving in the right flow.

Yes, there are bumps and snags along the road, but we have you.

We have the control.

We know what your client needs.

We know what your nature is, so we blend, and we mend and we hold the patterns.

For real.

Doubting still?

What a process, what a sign directly, the energy and the healing from divine.

Sit back and process the information you receive.

Do you really think we allow you or they to be deceived?

No, little sweet, we do not.

You just recognize what you are not.

You are not willing this to be done in your human form.

You are connected and open to the streams with no alarms.

Find joy, find peace and let go of sorrow.

Put your faith in the now and not what you may get done tomorrow.

Jackie: I just want to be the best healer I can be. I also want to be true and authentic.

Pluck the weeds of doubt out.

Do not overthink or project how you rank.

We are taking care of you, Ma.

We know how to pull the puppet strings to master the ring.

You're rejoicing once again.

Truth never dies, and we cannot be part of any lies.

We would not show ourselves, even in disguise.

The healings are real.

The work is true.

We celebrate every inch of you.

When you think you're doing it wrong, Ma, that's when we come along.

Ma, we do not expect perfection, for there is no such thing.

Human you are, and therefore humanness you bring.

Let us work on your behalf, and do not fret over who pours the water in your glass.

Just drink it up and say your praise.

Drink it up and rejoice in your day.

Pluck the weeds out.

Pluck the weeds out.

Replace doubt and fear by drawing us near.

Jackie: Thank you, thank you, thank you. I love you all so much.

## A Prayer for the Doubting Healer from Devyne and the We

Me as a Healer: I don't know if what I felt was real.

The We: We move through feeling, not logic. Trust the whisper.

Me as a Healer: What if I'm not good enough to help?

The We: It is not your "goodness" that heals, but your willingness to show up.

Me as a Healer: Maybe I'm making it up.

The We: You are tuning in, not making up. Truth has always worn your voice.

Me as a Healer: I feel small in the presence of others.

The We: Then stand in our presence. We are always with you.

Me as a Healer: I want to be a true and authentic healer.

The We: Then be honest about your doubt and let love answer it.

## Who Am I Really?

Jackie, dearest little one,

You are pure love.

You are the epitome of compassion.

You are whole.

You are amazing.

You are valued beyond measure.

You are made from the stars.

You are the stars.

You dream in the realm of the stars.

You know yourself as divine.

You live and remain outside of time.

Do not let the precious body fool you, make you think you are this and nothing else.

Resist the heaviness.

Allow your cream to float to the top.

You are not tied to this play.

You are everywhere, exploring every day.

You are the precious with the soul of mission.

Your mission feels extreme, but here's the thing:

You rely on much more than your earthly thoughts.

We have your back.

We do not wane.

The stars, the planet, they align, and your destiny stays in the same.

So help you request this here:

Do not fear, fret, worry, hate, or mourn.

We are here.


## MESSAGE FOR CARD 19 – RELIC OF TIME

Q: Devyne, what is the message for card 19, Relic of Time?

A: Ma, Be kind to yourself.

Be faithful of yourself.

You owe nobody anything, and you have nothing to prove.

You have more time than you can imagine.

Life that sounds the hourglass is just an illusion.

Play your role well, but remember to tell the fact from the fiction.

Detach from false narratives.

You have the gift, the strength, and the joy to use all of your toys to make changes, in self and in others, and have fun doing it.

# ABOUT THE AUTHOR

## JACKIE SUZANNE RUBIO

Jackie Suzanne Rubio has been through hell and somehow, she's still standing. She's faced the murder of her son, Devyne, the betrayal of court systems that failed her, and the gut-wrenching loss of contact with her grandson. Life has thrown the worst at her, over and over, and yet here she is, fierce, loving, compassionate, and still kicking.

She knows firsthand that life is messy, unfair, and sometimes downright cruel. She's a recovering alcoholic, a single mother, and a woman who has stumbled, screamed, cried, and yes, cussed her way through the chaos. But she's also learned something powerful: love doesn't care how broken or lost you are. Your connections with the people you care about, dead or alive, will find a way to reach you, no matter what.

Jackie's story isn't about perfection. She'll throw a fit in traffic, swear like a sailor, and sometimes feel like the world is against her, but she also wakes up every day ready to heal, to grow, and to help others walk through their own hell. She does it with bold honesty, in-your-face energy, and a whole lot of heart, showing readers that even when life is messy and chaotic, love, guidance, and connection are never out of reach.

Her journey led her into Reiki, quantum healing, intuitive abilities, automatic writing, and energy work, not as a hobby, but as a lifeline, a way to navigate the impossible, and a way to show others that connection, hope, and love are always possible. Jackie teaches people to trust their intuition, embrace the messiness of life, and open themselves to guidance that can't be ignored. She does it with fierce honesty and bold energy, but always from a place of deep compassion and unwavering love, her no-nonsense approach is her way of holding space, showing up fully, and letting people know they are never alone, no matter how hard life hits.

Through *From Murder to Messages*, Jackie holds out her hand and says, "I know grief. I know loss. I know betrayal. And I'll walk with you anyway." Her life is proof that even when the world tries to break you, you can rise, laugh, love, and live fully. She shows that no matter how far down the scale you've fallen, love and connection always find a way, and that even in the darkest moments, there's a hand ready to guide you back to the light.

*Jackie's Linktree*

www.ingramcontent.com/pod-product-compliance
Lightning Source LLC
LaVergne TN
LVHW051232080426
835513LV00016B/1544